D1457396

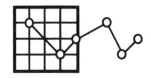

THE INSIDER'S GUIDE TO DEMOGRAPHIC KNOW-HOW

Everything marketers need to know about how to find, analyze and use information about their customers.

EDITED BY

Penelope Wickham

AMERICAN DEMOGRAPHICS PRESS
Ithaca, NY

THE INSIDER'S GUIDE TO
DEMOGRAPHIC KNOW-HOW

American Demographics Press
A Division of American Demographics, Inc.
108 N. Cayuga Street, Ithaca, NY 14850

ISBN 0-936889-03-9
Library of Congress Catalog Number 88-22136

LIBRARY OF CONGRESS CATALOGING IN PUBLICATION DATA

Wickham, Penelope, 1949-
The insider's guide to demographic know-how.

ISBN 0-936889-03-9

Printed in the United States of America.

Designed by Anne Kilgore

Compositor: James Madden

TABLE OF CONTENTS

CHAPTER 5—FEDERAL AGENCIES

FEDERAL GOVERNMENT SOURCES

The government has more data than most people realize. Federal agencies offer a plethora of data and projections at the national level. The advantage of these data is that they are collected by the government and are probably the most accurate. They are also relatively inexpensive.

SUBJECT CONTACTS AT FEDERAL AGENCIES

A quick reference guide and useful directory of subject specialists in the federal government agencies.

CHAPTER 6—STATE AND LOCAL SOURCES

STATE AND LOCAL SOURCES

In addition to state-level information on population and vital statistics, these organizations can often provide data for counties and cities. Many state sources have computer capabilities to do custom analysis of government data for you.

CHAPTER 7—NONPROFIT ORGANIZATIONS

NONPROFIT SOURCES OF DEMOGRAPHIC DATA

Nonprofit organizations are a disparate group. Some have detailed projections similar to those of private data companies; others conduct surveys and compile data on subjects that are not found elsewhere.

CHAPTER 8—PRIVATE FIRMS

PRIVATE SOURCES OF DEMOGRAPHIC DATA AND RELATED SERVICES

Private firms are usually the best source for current estimates and projections of small geographic areas. They often combine demographic indicators with consumer media and purchase behavior. Turnaround time is usually immediate for this information. However, it can be expensive.

APPENDIX

PREFACE

If you're intrigued by demographic analysis, but always thought you had to wear a green eyeshade to figure out how to use it in your work, then this is the book for you. It tells you how to understand and start using demographic analysis, and gives you up-to-date, detailed information about the various sources of demographic data.

This is also the book for you if you are a whiz at demographic research and know how to evaluate the accuracy of projections, understand the difference between cluster analysis and psychographics, and can talk easily about centroids and polygons. *The Insider's Guide* is designed so that you can quickly skim the chapters and pluck out only the information you need.

Demographic analysis is simply the process of painting a statistical portrait of your customers. Once you know what they "look" like—how old they are, whether they're married or not, how much they make, what their households are like, what they buy, where they live, what magazines they read—you can figure out what products they're most likely to want, and determine how to get your sales message across to them.

It used to be easy. Back in the '50s, everyone knew that the typical American family was composed of Dad at work, Mom at home, and two kids in school, and that what the Jones family bought, the Smith family bought too. But nowadays, the Joneses are likely to be divorced, the Smiths may be childless, and both Mrs.—or rather, Ms.—Smith and Ms. Jones are in the workforce. The products and services they want are as different as their individual situations, with the result that what was once one big, happy market is now broken up into many distinct segments. Today the most profitable firm is the firm that pinpoints and responds to market changes. This is the function of demographic analysis.

HOW TO USE THIS BOOK

1. Getting started Part I is a step-by-step guide to the basics of demographic analysis: why it's important, how to analyze the numbers, and how to actually buy data and research services. These articles will convince you that demographic analysis is not as formidable as it sometimes appears to the uninitiated.

2. Getting the information Part II is the heart of this book. It details almost 600 federal, state, local, nonprofit, and private sources of demographic data and related services. In it, you'll learn what each source has to offer, the name and phone number of who you should call for more information or to place an order, and, where available, prices. It includes an extensive list of subject contacts, complete with phone numbers, of over 300 specialists at the Census Bureau and other federal agencies, an elusive and, until now, hard-to-locate group.

Tips that will help you make a purchase decision about demographic data, mapping software, psychographic research, marketing services, demographically-enhanced mailing lists, and forecasts are also included.

3. The appendix offers a rich assortment of helpful information: a demographic profile of the United States; a list of useful directories, publications, and other guides; an extensive glossary of terms; and a subject index.

I would like to thank Martha Farnsworth Riche and Diane Crispell, editor/publisher and associate editor, respectively, of *The Numbers News*, and the authors of the original version, and basis, of this book; Margaret Ambry, who provided the all-important technical guidance; Cheryl Russell, editor-in-chief of *American Demographics*, the magazine that started it all; Jim Madden, who did much of the legwork and almost all of the production; Anne Kilgore, the designer and publishing advisor; and everyone else at American Demographics, especially Gary Graziano, Jerri Dougherty, and, last but not least, Peter Francese.

WHY YOU NEED DEMOGRAPHICS

THE FOLLOWING ARTICLES, WHICH ORIGINALLY appeared in *American Demographics* magazine, outline why demographic analysis is so important to any examination of your market.

HOW TO MANAGE CONSUMER INFORMATION

by Peter Francese

Here's the step-by-step way to knowing exactly who your customers are, what they want, and how to wrap it all up into a spectacular target marketing program.

The sea of consumer information is now at high tide. There are at least 70 firms that make it their business to provide researchers with information about consumer markets. With so many demographic, psychographic, media use, and purchasing behavior statistics around, planners and researchers need to know how to manage them, just like lottery winners need to know how to manage their money. Such newly rich must research the many investment alternatives and then match their investments with their need for financial security, additional income, and asset growth.

In the same way, business people should manage consumer information by researching alternative sources of data and matching what is available with their firm's need for securing market share through effective advertising, for creating additional income by increasing the market penetration of their products, and for generating corporate growth through the development of successful new products and services. The volume of consumer information has grown enormously in the past 15 years partly because the mass market has splintered into many market segments, each of which must be tracked by businesses selling to those segments. At the same time, the cost of buying and processing consumer data has fallen. It is now far cheaper to buy data about the characteristics of a market segment or a potential store site than to have a new product or a new store fail.

There are many reasons why consumer product and service companies buy information, but they fall into four main categories: (1) market management, (2) product analysis, (3) advertising strategy, and (4) strategic planning.

Market management involves the assessment of market potential in each geographic area, the allocation of sales territories by market potential, and the choosing of sites for sales outlets or distribution points.

Product or service analysis involves calculating a product's market potential as well as the manufacturer's market share, determining the characteristics of the people who most often buy the product or service (the prime market segments), and assessing the amount of the product or service, in units or dollars, that is purchased by each market segment.

Advertising strategy involves selecting the most cost-effective media (TV, radio, print, or direct mail), allocating an advertising budget among competing broadcasters or publishers, and developing a message that will be most effective at getting the consumer's attention and selling the goods.

Strategic planning involves tracking the growth or decline of existing markets, finding new growth markets, and determining what new or existing products are most likely to be successful in those markets.

Each of these activities requires the analysis of consumer information. Most consumer product companies have large budgets for buying data. But after several years of data gathering, a business can end up with a chaotic collection of data files, each purchased to solve an immediate problem. With an understanding of how to manage consumer information, however, businesses can create an integrated consumer information system that matches assorted data files with an array of research needs.

VISUALIZING THE FLOW

Where does all this information come from? People do four things that generate information (see figure 1). First, people answer the census every ten years. In addition, each March a random sample of

Figure 1

THE COMPLETE CONSUMER

Consumers generate four types of information of importance to businesses. By linking this information together, companies can build a complete picture of the consumer.

about 50,000 householders answers the demographic questionnaire included in the Current Population Survey. These two sources provide the basic demographic information about consumers—their age, sex, race, income, education, occupation, and household structure. Demographic information is essential to businesses as they attempt to project the demand for products such as toys, lawn care supplies, and retirement homes, a demand that is determined by the age, household structure, and income distribution of the population.

As essential as they are, however, demographics are not enough. Two people, both aged 40, both with incomes of $50,000 a year, will want different products depending on their lifestyle. That's why one of them will buy a Mercedes and the other a Winnebago. Both products meet the need for transportation, but each product satisfies a different want—the one a desire for status, the other a desire for recreation.

By responding to surveys, consumers provide researchers with this second type of information: a psychographic profile. A business must know how consumers feel about themselves and the world around them to effectively communicate their product's ability to satisfy consumers' wants and needs.

The third way that consumers generate information is by revealing through monitoring devices and surveys what they watch on TV, what they listen to on the radio, and what newspapers and magazines they read. Nielsen and Arbitron, for example, find out who watches what TV shows and who listens to what radio stations, while Simmons Market Research Bureau and Mediamark Research determine who reads what magazines or newspapers.

Fourth, consumers, by definition, spend money. This also generates information. Every time people use a credit card, the slip of paper that they sign becomes a statistic about a purchase. Every time someone in a test market panel buys groceries in a scanner-equipped store, he or she generates another purchase statistic. Panel diary firms and the Census Bureau through the Consumer Expenditure Survey also collect data on purchasing by asking householders to keep track of everything they buy for several weeks. All of these purchase statistics help a packaged goods company measure how well its advertising is working.

THE UNBROKEN CIRCLE

There is more to the flow of consumer information than these four segments—demographics, psychographics, media use, and purchasing behavior—because it is the combination of these statistics that creates a statistical picture of the consumer. Demographics in combination with psychographics, for example, can tell what certain people want from a product. A researcher can find out what Yuppies want from a suit of clothes or what the elderly want from financial services.

Demographics in combination with purchasing data can tell a food retailer or bakery firm who buys whole what bread, how much of it they buy, how many potential buyers there are now, and how many there will be in the future.

Psychographics and purchasing behavior together explain, for example, why people buy mail-order products and what advertisers should say in their promotional efforts to get people to buy more.

Media preferences, in combination with demographics and purchasing behavior, tell advertisers and advertising agencies how consumers get information, with what media consumers can be most efficiently reached, and how much it will cost to reach consumers who play golf or gamble in the futures market.

A growing number of companies are now offering hybrids of consumer information based on these four types of data. SRI International and Yankelovich Clancy Shulman, for example, provide psychographic profiles of consumers in combination with demographic statistics. They offer age and income profiles of attitudes and lifestyle groups. By asking consumers about purchasing behavior and media use, both SRI and Yankelovich Clancy Shulman also offer psychographic profiles of, for example, people who watch a lot of daytime television or who eat white bread.

Mediamark Research, Inc. and Simmons Market Research Bureau ask about 20,000 adults each year detailed questions about what magazines and newspapers they read, what TV shows they watch, and which radio stations they listen to. But MRI and SMRB also ask, and then cross-tabulate, demographic questions such as age, income, occupation, education, residence, and household type, as well as questions about the products and services that consumers recently purchased. These firms then combine their media use data with psychographic profiles to provide a more complete picture of, for example, who reads *Money* magazine.

Nielsen and Arbitron monitor the broadcast industry to see which stations reach the largest proportion of households. But Nielsen also collects data from store audits to track consumer purchasing behavior. And Arbitron recently introduced an in-home scanning device which combines purchasing behavior with exposure to broadcast advertising.

Finally, the Consumer Expenditure Survey and syndicated panel diaries (National Family Opinion, NPD Research) link information on purchasing directly with demographics.

PIECES OF THE PUZZLE

A complete consumer information system should contain the four types of consumer-generated data along with some way of linking the demographic, psychographic, media use, and purchasing statistics, as shown in figure 1. Every business may not need every piece of the puzzle; it depends on the kind of business it is and what research activities—market analysis, product analysis, advertising, or strategic planning—it is involved in (see figure 2). For each purpose, some pieces

Figure 2

PUTTING CONSUMER INFORMATION TO WORK

Companies use consumer information for four purposes. Demographics and purchasing behavior are important to all four, while psychographics and media preferences are important for advertising.

	DEMOGRAPHICS	PSYCHOGRAPHICS	MEDIA PREFERENCES	PURCHASING BEHAVIOR
MARKET ANALYSIS	●			●
PRODUCT ANALYSIS	●			●
ADVERTISING	●	●	●	●
STRATEGIC PLANNING	●			●

of data are more important than others.

For market management, the most important piece is demographic, because it is the most readily available data for small geographic areas. Purchasing behavior is also important to market managers so that they can determine the amount of potential business by zip code or census tract. Psychographic and media data are less important to market analysis, partly because they do not describe the volume of consumption and because they are not available for small areas.

For product analysis, both demographic and purchasing behavior are important. These two pieces of information identify important market segments and determine how well they are being served.

Reaching consumers efficiently with a convincing message about a product or service requires the greatest amount of information. Designing an ad message involves psychographics and demographics; choosing between broadcast and print media requires statistics on media use and demographics, as does choosing particular stations or newspapers or magazines in which to run an ad. Perhaps this is why cluster analysis, which is a statistical way to combine much of this data, is so popular in advertising agencies.

For strategic planning, a business needs demographic projections combined with statistics on purchasing behavior. Strategic planners use this information to predict such things as the future market for four-wheel drive vehicles. Data on lifestyles and media preferences are less useful to strategic planners because lifestyles and the media can change unpredictably.

There are other issues of importance in gauging what information a business needs, such as the accuracy and timeliness of data, but these factors are secondary to the main question: How does it all fit together? Consider this model of consumer information as data processing software for the mind.

HOW TO SIZE UP YOUR CUSTOMERS

by Marvin Nesbit and Arthur Weinstein

To survive in today's competitive environment, you must find and exploit your niche by systematically identifying the distinct market segments into which your customers fall.

Retailers have long depended on their ability to size up their customers when they walk in the door. Customers give themselves away by their clothing, speech, mannerisms, and body language. While gut instinct still works for some retailers, the era of successful scrutiny has passed. You can no longer pigeonhole at a glance because the increasing diversity of consumers has made such stereotyping futile. Today you need a more systematic way to understand your customers.

Some managers are skeptical about the effectiveness of demographics in defining distinct markets because no single demographic variable explains buyer behavior. There are exceptions, of course—new parents buy diapers; Minnesotans buy winter coats. While it usually takes more than demographic knowledge to understand a market, the demographics should not be ignored for several reasons.

First, demographic information is the most accessible and cost-effective way to identify a target market, and it is within practically everyone's budget. Even if demographic statistics are a less than perfect marketing tool, they frequently can provide you with a competitive edge.

Second, demographic variables are good indicators of purchasing behavior for many broad product and service categories. While they cannot predict brand choice, most businesses are more concerned with product choice than brand choice.

Third, demographic variables reveal ongoing trends—such as shifts in age distribution and household types. These trends can create new market segments and provide a business with opportunities that could be profitable.

Fourth, businesses can use demographics to evaluate their marketing efforts. A business can compare internal sales records with the demographics of its target markets—for example, readjusting its marketing strategies to reflect changing market demographics.

THE FOUR Rs

Is it worthwhile to segment your market? To decide, you should ask yourself four key questions. If you answer "yes" to these questions, then segmenting your market is worth pursuing. We call these criteria the Four Rs.
• Can you *rank* your target markets by their importance to your overall market?
• Are your target markets of *realistic* size, large enough to profitably pursue?
• Can you *reach* your targeted customers easily?
• Will your targeted customers *respond* to marketing strategies?

CAN YOU RANK YOUR TARGET MARKETS?

You must evaluate, both objectively and subjectively, the potential of one target market relative to another in order to decide which one is worth pursuing. To do this, you need to quantify your total market and each of its segments.

Demographics can be an effective tool for measuring markets. One client of Florida University's Small Business Development Center—a dentist—wanted to specialize in cosmetic dentistry, including bonding, implants, and related aesthetic services. But he didn't know whether the market for cosmetic dentistry in his service area was large enough to be worth pursuing as a specialization. We knew that potential cosmetic dentistry patients were professionals, managers, and administrators near their earnings peak. Most prime candidates for cosmetic dentistry have discretionary income.

Using cluster analysis, we determined the size of the overall dentistry market in his area, then zeroed in on the potential market for cosmetic dentistry. The cluster analysis included such variables as household income, age distribution, homeownership, and education.

We found six potential dental market segments in the area. We ranked as potentially profitable for cosmetic dentistry three segments, the Up and Comers, American Dream, and Home Base, primarily because of their size and income level. A fourth segment, The Condo Dwellers, could have been profitable, but its small size made the cost of reaching this market too expensive to pursue. We considered unprofitable for cosmetic dentistry the remaining two segments, Opa-Locka (a low-income area), and the Squeezed Seniors, in part because of their income levels but also because of their distance from the dental office.

Our research indicated that only 10 percent of this dentist's service-area population were prime candidates for cosmetic dentistry. Even if cosmetic dentistry were a well-known specialization, the potential market, according to the cluster analysis, was small. Two other dental markets were larger than cosmetic dentistry—preventive and preventive-remedial dentistry, accounting for more than 44 percent of the dentist's market potential.

IS THE TARGETED MARKET REALISTIC IN SIZE?

Each market that you target must be large enough to support the cost of the marketing effort. You should consider both the number of potential customers and their incomes in order to estimate the purchasing power of the segment.

Another client of the Center wanted to open a day-care center; she needed to find the best site for it. We identified three potential sites for the center using demographic information from the Census Bureau, looking for census tracts in which a large number of working mothers with children under age six lived. We also plotted the existing day-care centers in a map, together with the population density of working mothers. This competitive analysis supplemented the demographic data and helped assess the feasibility of the venture.

The map pinpointed the areas that had at least 2,500 mothers in the labor force with children under six and no existing day-care center. The final site selection was done by the client, choosing only among the best locations.

CAN YOU REACH THE TARGETED CUSTOMERS?

Your targeted customers should be readily accessible. For market segmentation to work effectively, you have to be able to reach distinct markets through select media and targeted messages. The higher cost of reaching a distinct market must be justified by higher sales to that market.

You can use demographics to identify the media that reach your target markets most efficiently. Once you have a demographic profile of your customers, you can compare it with the readership profile of a newspaper, the listenership profile of a radio station, or the zip code demographics that you will reach through direct mail. Even if a perfect match is impossible, your business can gain a competitive edge by knowing how your targeted customers' demographics match with the media you are using to reach them.

You can also use the demographic profile of your targeted customers to design your promotional campaigns and advertising. We developed a cost-effective promotional plan, based on demographic information, for a minority-owned Goodyear automotive franchise owner. First we examined the franchise owner's market, finding that it was a relatively poor, black neighborhood with a youthful population and rapid population turnover. Based on these demographics and the experiences of similar businesses, we recommended that the company use coupons, special offers, premiums, and contests in its promotions to stimulate new business. We also suggested that these promotions be directed at the black population through local radio stations and newspapers. We encouraged the franchise to sponsor special promotional events. One such event, a car-care clinic especially for women, proved successful.

If the targeted customers don't respond to your marketing efforts, you shouldn't be marketing to them. Thorough market research, including surveys of noncustomers as well as customers, can help you identify whether potential customers need your particular product or service before you spend money trying to sell to them.

Demographics, combined with market survey research, can identify potentially responsive market segments. One Small Business Development Center client had a retail office supply business that was declining in a changing neighborhood. At first he thought he needed to relocate in order to make his business grow. But after relocating, his sales continued to lag.

We analyzed his new trading area, using data from the local county planning department. The analysis revealed a large concentration of school-aged children in his trade area. Further research indicated that sales of school supplies, which peaked in September, represented a significant business opportunity for him. Sales to small businesses located in his new market area represented another opportunity.

The retailer changed his merchandising mix, store hours, and promotional strategies to better meet the needs of the area. The small businesses needed custom office products and computer-related supplies. The school age population needed economical and attractive school supplies. After implementing the changes, his sales jumped 300 percent in the first year. In September alone the store increased its sales of school supplies 16-fold.

Smart managers know that when they size up their customers, appearances can be deceiving. Demographics are also sometimes deceiving, but at least you can go back for a second look.

FOUR TIPS

If, after analyzing the Four Rs, you decide that it might be profitable to segment your market, here are a few tips that should help you.

1. GET THE DEMOGRAPHIC INFORMATION YOU NEED FOR DECISION MAKING. The first step in demographic analysis is planning. You need actionable information, not just numbers. Any information you collect should help you solve specific marketing problems. First determine what you already know about your customers. Then determine what else you need to know, isolating the demographic component of your information needs. Sources of demographic data include local planning departments, state data centers, private data firms, and federal statistical offices. The local public library might be the best place to begin.

2. USE RELEVANT DEMOGRAPHIC VARIABLES. One or two demographic variables, such as age and income, may not be enough. Demographic data include education levels, household types, marital status, occupation, and so on. Cluster analysis, a technique that classifies neighborhoods by statistically grouping demographic variables that are linked to one another, may be useful for some businesses.

3. USE DEMOGRAPHICS TO ENHANCE—NOT REPLACE—INTUITION. Despite the value of research, you shouldn't ignore your gut instincts about your customers. Demographic information can add insight to your instincts, stimulating you to market more creatively. Demographic change is the result of many social, economic, and cultural trends, and demographic information can give you a context for understanding how your customers are changing.

4. USE CENSUS INFORMATION, CURRENT ESTIMATES, AND PROJECTIONS. A market changes as the people who live there change. The 1980 census will give you the historical information about your area that will help you understand the ongoing change. You also need up-to-date information on the local area, available from your state data center, your county planning department, or from private data companies. In addition, local area projections—available from state data centers or from private data companies—can give you a look into the future, aiding you in long-range business planning.

HOW TO THINK LIKE A DEMOGRAPHER

by Thomas Exter

It's a simple way to look at the world. Populations and markets are the same kind of beast.

Demographers and marketers both view the world in simple terms. One studies populations; the other studies markets. When populations grow too fast, demographers try to slow them down. When markets grow too slowly, marketers try to speed them up. When marketers think like demographers, they gain an understanding of how things work that can help them increase market size, deepen market penetration, and carve out market share.

Births, deaths, and migration are the only things that change a population's size. In marketing, a "birth" occurs when someone wants a product or service. The market for automobiles grows, for example, when more people want a new car. Like the birthrate, the rate at which people need a new car can rise or fall for many reasons, including demographic and economic ones.

Advertising can increase the demand for new cars, especially if the cars have features that drivers want, such as lengthy warranties. Kodak promotes births in its market with advertising that encourages camera buffs to take more pictures—regardless of the brand of film they use. As the dominant company in the field, Kodak gains when it increases the size of the total market.

"Mortality" in the film market occurs when people stop taking pictures. The automobile market loses people when they give up driving. Advertising can postpone mortality and encourage fertility by emphasizing the fun of picture-taking and the features on the latest cars.

When people move to a new city, like Los Angeles, they enter a network of jobs, housing developments, retail establishments, and freeways. When consumers enter the automobile market, they open themselves to sales pitches, advertisements, and to noticing their neighbor's car. Once in the market, their decision-making centers on what brand to buy. Brand selection and brand switching are analogous to migration.

Most demographers agree that the population policies that are hardest to make work are those that try to influence migration. Likewise, brand managers would probably agree that it is hardest to influence brand switching. Advertising can create brand awareness and reinforce brand images, but rarely does it cause brand switching.

MARKET SNAPSHOTS

Since populations are always changing , the only way to measure a population is by stopping the clock. On April 1, 1990 the Census Bureau will count every head in the country and measure our population's size, distribution, and composition.

Market researchers also need to stop the clock to calculate the size, distribution, and composition of their markets. Market researchers rely on consumer surveys to estimate these characteristics. Just as computer technology has revolutionized the decennial population census, technologies like people meters and UPC scanners are changing the collection and analysis of consumer information. But the growing sophistication of data collection should not obscure the common purpose of population censuses and consumer surveys. Both attempt to measure people at one point in time in order to describe their characteristics and calculate how they are changing.

The composition of a population or a market includes people's age, sex, income, educational attainment, occupation, and ethnicity. Population and market composition changes because of births, deaths, and migration. Market composition also changes as people's needs and desires for products shift. Young people may buy more computers at first, but as older people catch on, they also become important to the computer market. High-income innovators may buy microwave ovens initially, but as prices fall a broader spectrum of people buy them. Consumer surveys keep companies on top of the changing composition of their markets.

The distribution of a market depends on consumer geography and technology. Consumers can be part of a market as long as products and services can reach them. New channels of product distribution emerge with new technologies. From walk-in retail outlets to direct marketing by mail, telephone, television, and computer, distribution channels determine the distribution of a market. Marketers in search of an optimal distribution network for their products must consider not only the distribution of the population, but also the efficiency of their market channels.

Brand managers who want to increase the size of their total market need to attract customers to the product category (promote births), retain current customers (prevent deaths), and convert customers of the competition to their brand (encourage migration). A new product will require investing resources in attracting new customers to the product category as well as to the brand. A mature product will require investing resources to increase product use and to point out strategic brand differences.

How to Analyze the Numbers

DEMOGRAPHIC ANALYSIS CAN BE AS EASY AS PICKING up your pocket calculator. The following pieces, reprinted from *American Demographics* magazine, give you step-by-step guidelines to the basics of consumer research.

How To Do Demographic Analysis on A Hand-Held Calculator

by Michael J. Batutis

Here's a step-by-step guide to doing demographic analysis on a hand-held calculator. You'll be surprised at how easy it is.

Some people picture demographers as moles with computers who burrow deeply into vast data files. While many government and academic demographers do live in such surroundings, there are simpler ways to do demographic analysis.

Most demographic analysis is a matter of applying straightforward, simple calculations. This article takes you step-by-step through some common demographic measures you can calculate with a hand-held calculator. Learning these techniques will help free you from reliance on printed tables, which not only appear after the data on computer tape but also may not contain the numbers you want.

Please note that I made no attempt to use a "representative" calculator. My aim is to illustrate the simple arithmetic functions available on even the most basic of pocket calculators. Demographic analysis does not necessarily require a programmable calculator, or one with sophisticated scientific functions.

RATIOS

The most common calculation used in demographic analysis is the ratio. A ratio is a measure that expresses the relative size of two numbers. It comes in three forms, each slightly different.

• The form $a \div b$, where "a" and "b" are numbers from the same population, or universe. Examples of such a ratio include the sex ratio (men divided by women), and the dependency ratio (workers divided by nonworkers). In each example, both the numerator and denominator of the ratio refer to the population in a specific geographic area, for example the United States, a state, or region.

• The ratio a ÷ b, where "a" and "b" are numbers from different universes. Examples of this type include population density (population divided by land area), average household size (people living in households divided by the number of households), and per capita income (income divided by population).

• The special ratio called a proportion, a ÷ (a+b), where "a" and "b" are from the same universe, such as the proportion of households that contain married couples (married-couple households divided by all households, including married-couple households), or the proportion of the population that is black. This type of ratio relates the size of "a" to the size of some larger quantity in which "a" is included. This ratio has properties not shared by the other types of ratios. Its value ranges from zero to one and, if multiplied by 100, becomes a percentage.

People who work with demographic statistics often use rates, which are another kind of ratio. Strictly defined, a rate is the number of occurrences of an event, such as deaths, divided by the population at risk of dying. By this definition a death rate would relate the number of deaths in a population during some time period to the population at risk of dying during the same period. Such measures include birth rates, death rates, net migration rates, fertility rates, labor force participation rates, literacy rates, crime rates, divorce rates, and housing vacancy rates. (These measures, in reality, are ratios rather than rates because the "true" population at risk, which must be known to calculate a rate, is often difficult to identify. Demographers call these measures rates, however, by convention.)

ANALYZING DATA

With these ratios in mind and a calculator in hand, you are ready to tackle a printout of data from Summary Tape File 1-A for New York State. Most state data centers have printouts for their particular state from this summary tape, which provides statistics from the short-form census questionnaire. You can analyze the structure of the 1980 population and, by making comparisons with comparable printed reports from the 1970—and, when available, from the 1990—census, measure trends during the decade.

Table I contains the population by age and sex for New York State almost as it appears on STF 1-A. The number of males by age is not on the tape but is derived by subtracting females from the total population. The problem is that the tape file contains only counts, but not a percentage distribution by age, nor does it place the population in five-year groups, the conventional way to display age data. These numbers reveal a variety of things about the structure of the New York State population, however, once you do some simple analysis with a hand-held calculator.

Examining the composition of the population by age and sex requires the use of percents, or proportions. The formula for a proportion is a ÷ (a + b), and a percent is a proportion multiplied by 100. To calculate percent male, then, the formula is: percent males = (number of males ÷ total population) x 100.

On a calculator, using only the basic arithmetic functions, the sequence is:

Enter	Function	Display
8,339,422 *(males)*	÷	8,339,422
17,558,072 *(total population)*	x	0.4749623
100	=	47.49623

The percentage can be rounded to 47.5. The percentage of females can be calculated in the same way, by substituting the number of females for the number of males in the sequence above. The percent female can also be, of course, calculated by subtracting the percent male from 100. In either case the result is 52.5.

In 1970, males were 47.8 percent and females were 52.2 percent of the population. Overall, there was little change in the sex composition of New York's population between 1970 and 1980. However, there are now proportionately even more women than men at older ages, due primarily to increased life expectancy among elderly females.

Another measure of the sex composition of a population, the sex ratio, is also easy to calculate. The formula for the sex ratio is: (males ÷ females) x 100.

The sex ratio is defined as the number of males per 100 females. To calculate the ratio from the data in Table I do the following:

Table I: New York State Population by Age and Sex, 1980

(from the 1980 Census Summary Tape File 1-A)

Age	Total	Males	Females
< 1	240,554	122,502	118,052
1 & 2	450,033	230,304	219,729
3 & 4	445,338	227,583	217,755
5	221,874	113,693	108,181
6	217,071	110,553	106,518
7–9	745,934	381,300	364,634
10–13	1,106,292	564,656	541,636
14	299,768	152,348	147,420
15	315,775	160,721	155,054
16	323,055	164,079	158,976
17	322,169	163,299	158,870
18	314,983	157,062	157,921
19	322,589	158,478	164,111
20	314,719	153,957	160,762
21	307,969	149,822	158,147
22–24	897,258	433,777	463,481
25–29	1,428,376	690,997	737,379
30–34	1,351,839	649,344	702,495
35–44	2,043,219	973,142	1,070,077
45–54	1,908,113	902,353	1,005,760
55–59	979,370	456,018	523,352
60–61	354,865	162,885	191,980
62–64	486,142	219,617	266,525
65–74	1,292,428	541,851	750,577
75–84	675,356	241,135	434,221
85+	192,983	57,946	135,037
Total Pop.	17,558,072	8,339,422	9,218,650
Median Age	31.9	30.3	33.4

Enter	Function	Display
8,339,422 *(males)*	÷	8,339,422
9,218,650 *(females)*	x	0.9046225
100	=	90.46225

The rounded figure 90.5 is lower than the comparable 91.5 ratio from the 1970 census. According to table 17 of the PC(1)-B report from 1970, the sex ratio in New York has been declining since 1930, consistent with the national trend. This means men are a smaller share of the population than they used to be.

POPULATION SHIFTS

Just as important as age and sex composition is how a population is changing, which is usually expressed as percent change. The formula for percent change in population is: $((P_2 - P_1) \div P_1) \times 100$, where P_1 is the population at the initial point and P_2 is the population at a later point.

This equation is identical to: $(P_2 \div P_1) - 1.00 \times 100$, which is easier to apply on a calculator. To determine the percent change in population from 1970 to 1980, P_1 is the 1970 population and P_2 the 1980 population. To illustrate with data for New York:

Enter	Function	Display
17,558,072 *(1980 population)*	÷	17,558,072
18,241,391 *(1970 population)*	-	0.9625402
1.0	=	-0.0374598
	x	-0.0374598
100	=	-3.74598

Rounded to the nearest tenth, New York State's population declined 3.7 percent between 1970 and 1980.

The percent change in households can also be calculated with the same formula. In the 1970 census, the number of households enumerated in New York State was 5,913,861, and 6,340,429 in 1980. Using the same method then, the percent gain in households is 7.2.

How could the state with the largest decline in population between 1970 and 1980 (both in absolute numbers and in percent) have an increase of more than 7 percent in the number of households?

The calculator can help answer this question using statistics on the household population in 1970 and 1980. In 1970, there were 17,775,236 persons in households in New York State, and 17,107,975 persons in households in 1980. Since the number of persons in households has declined since 1970, the reason why the number of households has increased must lie elsewhere. Another ratio, average household size, or population per household, can be used to measure household change. The formula for this ratio is: population in households ÷ households.

To calculate average household size for 1970:

Enter	Function	Display
17,775,236 *(1970 population in households)*	÷	17,775,236
5,913,861 *(1970 households)*	=	3.0056905

There were 3.01 persons per household in 1970 in New York State, but only 2.70 in 1980. (Calculate the 1980 number using the 1980 household and population totals.)

Apply the percent change formula:

Enter	Function	Display
2.70 *(1980 average household size)*	÷	2.70
3.01 *(1970 average household size)*	-	0.89701
1.0	=	-0.10299
	x	-0.10299
100	=	-10.299

These calculations, then, reveal a 10.3 percent decline in average household size in New York State between 1970 and 1980. Since average household size declined faster during the seventies than either total population or population in households, the explanation for the decline in average household size must lie in changes in household composition. There must be proportionately more of the kinds of households that contain fewer people. But how can we be sure?

HOUSEHOLD TYPES

Table II shows the number of households in 1980 by type and size of household from STF 1-A. In 1980, there were 1,649,325 single-person households in

Table II: New York State Households by Household Type, and Sex of Householder, 1980
(from the 1980 Census Summary Tape File 1-A)

Persons in Household	Total	Male	Female
1 Person Hholds	1,649,325	631,323	1,018,002
2+ Person Hholds	—	—	—
Married Couple	3,445,743	—	—
Other Family	997,505	181,943	815,562
Non Family	247,856	142,445	105,411

New York State, compared to 1,194,544 recorded by the 1970 census, a 38.1 percent increase (the unrounded answer is 38.071516).

At the same time the number of married-couple households in New York State decline 10.2 percent since 1970 (there were 3,838,026 of them counted in 1970).

AGE STRUCTURE

You can calculate the change in the number of people in specific age groups, such as 20-to-29 year-olds. In 1970, there were 1,382,376 persons aged 20 to 24 in New York State, and 1,226,209 persons aged 25 to 29. To calculate the percent change for the 20-to-24 group, you must first combine age groups from Table I:

Enter	Function	Display
314,719 *(20-year-olds)*	+	314,719
307,969 *(21-year-olds)*	+	622,688
897,258 *(22-to-24-year-olds)*	=	1,519,946
	÷	1,519,946
1,382,376 *(20-to-24-year-olds in 1970)*	-	1.099517
1.0	=	0.099517
	x	0.099517
100	=	9.951706

The calculation for the 25-to-29 group is simpler because this age group appears in the printout. Calculate the 1970-1980 percentage change yourself (the answer is 16.487).

While the total population in New York State dropped 3.7 percent, then, there was a 10 percent increase in the 20-to-24 age group between 1970 and 1980 and a 16.5 percent increase in the 25-to-29 age group. The baby-boom generation is in the household-forming ages, and they appear to be forming single-person households at higher rates than previous generations.

OVERCOMING ANXIETY

These are only a few of the kinds of calculations that can be done on a pocket calculator. The point of doing such calculations, of course, is to study demographic change and to analyze population characteristics. Often, researchers have a specific problem in mind—to investigate the Hispanic market in Manhattan for example. To solve such problems the first step is to identify what you want to find out—Hispanic age structure, family composition, growth in population and households, and so forth.

The next step is to obtain the statistics. Census Bureau printed reports usually do not have all the statistics you need to solve specific problems because they are prepared with the general public in mind. They offer something for everybody, but rarely everything a single researcher is looking for. Many firms use private data companies to select the data they need from the census computer tapes.

The job of analysis remains. Before rushing to hire a high-priced analyst to do tabulations for you (on his hand-held calculator) you may find that not only can you do them yourself, but by educating yourself about the different demographic measures and performing the calculations, you may develop a more detailed understanding of the results.

How To Understand Tables

by Michael J. Batutis

Tables are only a collection of numbers arranged in a certain way, and you can unlock their often fascinating secrets by approaching them with a positive attitude and a simple four-step strategy.

Statistical tables suffer the reputation of being difficult to read, boring, and redundant. Doesn't the text point out all the interesting facts? Like footnotes and appendices, tables appear, many readers suspect, only to intimidate the reader—to prove that the author knows more about the subject than anybody else.

Nevertheless, statistical tables appear almost everywhere, from newspapers to trade journals. They come in many forms, from a single column of numbers to cross-classifications. Some readers ignore such tables, or give them only a glance. If you read an article without studying its accompanying table, however, you usually lose valuable information. The text that accompanies a table will make important points also covered in the table—but only those points that the author thinks are relevant.

You can tackle a table in all its complexity and detail by extracting its information one step at a time, building an understanding of the total table. This article takes you, one step at a time, through a table recently published by the Census Bureau: U.S. Bureau of the Census, Current Population Reports, P-60, No. 156, "Money Income of Households, Families, and Persons in the United States: 1985," U.S. Government Printing Office, Washington, D.C., 1987.

STEP ONE

Read the title of the table to understand what "universe" the data are drawn from and how that universe is cross-classified, or broken down. In the example, Table 6, the word "Households" in the title identifies the universe. The terms following the word "by" identify the variables by which the table classified households. This table presents information for the total number of households in the United States as of March, 1986, classified by the type of household, the household's total money income in 1985 and the race and Spanish origin of the householder. (For simplicity's sake we have not reproduced here the part of the table showing race and Spanish origin.)

The fine print below the title of Table 6 says that, unless otherwise indicated, all numbers in the table are in thousands. This means that all the numbers in the table have been rounded to the nearest thousand, and the numbers are understood to have three more zeros to the right of the last digit.

STEP TWO

After understanding the title, study the left-hand margin, which identifies the rows of the table, and the strip at the top of the table, which identifies the columns. The rows and columns divide the table into a matrix. Each cell of the matrix contains the number of households, rounded to the nearest thousand, in a specific type of family and income class. The words that describe each row and column indicate which category the number belongs to.

In addition, this table presents certain "derived" measures—median income, mean income, and per capita income. The table also shows standard errors of these derived measures, so that confidence intervals can be used with these measures.

STEP THREE

Having grasped the structure of the table, try to understand all the terms used in the table. If necessary, refer to the section of the report or the article that contains these definitions. In the case of the Current Population Reports the definitions are always in an appendix at the end of the report.

If you have any questions about what income is included in "total money income," or if you do not know the difference between "family" and "non-family" households, consult the definitions before you study the numbers. Many a false conclusion has resulted from a misunderstanding of a table's categories.

STEP FOUR

Only after you understand what information is displayed, what units of measurement are used, how the data are structured, and what all the terms mean should you tackle the numbers themselves. Start with the totals. The top row of numbers in Table 6 shows that of "all households"—the 88 million households estimated from the March 1986 Current Population Survey—63 million were family households, and 25 million were non-family households. (This sentence rounds the numbers in the table to the nearest million, a common practice in texts—another reason you should read tables.)

Think of the relationship these numbers imply: There were 2.5 family households for each non-family household.

Table 6. Type of Household—Households, by Total Money Income in 1985, Race, and Hispanic Origin of Householder

(NUMBERS IN THOUSANDS. HOUSEHOLDS AS OF MARCH 1986. FOR MEANING OF SYMBOLS, SEE TEXT)

TOTAL MONEY INCOME	ALL HOUSE-HOLDS	FAMILY HOUSEHOLDS				NONFAMILY HOUSEHOLDS						
		TOTAL	TYPE OF FAMILY			TOTAL	SINGLE-PERSON HOUSEHOLD			MULTIPLE-PERSON HOUSEHOLD		
			MARRIED COUPLE	MALE HOUSE-HOLDER-WIFE ABSENT	FEMALE HOUSE-HOLDER-HUSBAND ABSENT		TOTAL	SEX OF PERSON		TOTAL	SEX OF HOUSEHOLDER	
								MALE	FEMALE		MALE	FEMALE
ALL RACES												
TOTAL	88,458	63,558	50,933	2,414	10,211	24,900	21,178	8,285	12,893	3,722	2,363	1,359
UNDER $2,500	2,150	1,177	532	74	571	973	945	412	533	76	16	11
$2,500 TO $4,999	4,634	1,770	571	78	1,122	2,864	2,803	652	2,151	60	27	33
$5,000 TO $7,499	6,017	2,672	1,365	107	1,150	3,395	3,298	877	2,426	96	58	39
$7,500 TO $9,999	4,980	2,685	1,619	144	922	2,295	2,103	634	1,469	192	132	60
$10,000 TO $12,499	5,329	3,256	2,292	115	849	2,073	1,910	721	1,169	163	104	58
$12,500 TO $14,999	4,820	3,180	2,373	131	676	1,640	1,454	543	910	187	108	79
$15,000 TO $17,499	4,676	3,403	2,346	158	700	1,595	1,384	586	798	211	148	63
$17,500 TO $19,999	4,833	3,226	2,496	119	611	1,451	1,215	521	694	236	143	93
$20,000 TO $22,499	4,005	3,500	2,772	179	549	1,333	1,104	505	599	229	150	79
$22,500 TO $24,999	3,078	3,028	2,417	138	472	977	795	360	435	183	103	72
$25,000 TO $27,499	4,407	3,374	2,789	155	380	1,083	878	477	401	205	110	95
$27,500 TO $29,999	3,635	2,912	2,455	106	351	724	583	282	301	141	79	62
$30,000 TO $32,499	3,946	3,110	2,672	112	326	836	614	390	224	222	166	56
$32,500 TO $34,999	3,019	2,548	2,548	84	233	471	315	185	130	156	98	55
$35,000 TO $37,499	3,253	2,714	2,343	100	271	540	377	220	158	162	101	61
$37,500 TO $39,999	2,486	2,178	1,944	91	143	308	187	107	79	121	76	45
$40,000 TO $44,999	4,636	4,090	4,652	115	262	607	345	222	127	262	137	125
$45,000 TO $49,999	3,572	3,130	2,655	95	181	442	223	142	81	219	161	58
$50,000 TO $59,999	5,205	4,647	4,301	149	202	558	321	221	100	237	156	81
$60,000 TO $74,999	5,929	4,550	4,336	79	135	379	154	100	54	225	156	69
$75,000 AND OVER	3,927	3,570	3,373	92	105	357	170	132	38	187	134	54
MEDIAN INCOME.....DOLLARS.	23,618	28,072	31,161	24,354	14,316	13,798	11,884	16,312	9,774	28,773	30,043	27,744
STANDARD ERROR...DOLLARS.	128	149	145	612	257	166	131	267	133	746	761	774
MEAN INCOME......DOLLARS.	29,066	33,182	36,330	29,096	18,367	18,559	15,997	20,124	13,345	33,138	33,725	32,119
STANDARD ERROR...DOLLARS.	115	143	164	664	220	152	141	277	160	508	630	855
INCOME PER CHILD. MEMBER...DOLS.	10,884	10,235	11,072	9,908	5,902	15,313	15,997	20,124	13,345	13,702	13,665	13,772
MEAN SIZE OF HOUSEHOLD...	2.67	3.24	3.28	2.94	3.11	1.21	1.00	1.00	1.00	2.42	2.47	2.33
NUMBER WITH EARNINGS..THOUSANDS.	69,864	54,469	44,428	2,132	7,908	15,395	11,867	6,174	5,694	3,578	2,260	1,768
MEDIAN EARNINGS........DOLLARS.	25,284	27,600	30,764	23,304	13,938	17,991	16,319	18,675	14,060	27,357	28,416	25,878
STANDARD ERROR........DOLLARS.	117	161	140	585	281	203	176	312	277	674	962	990
MEAN EARNINGS.........DOLLARS.	29,323	31,600	34,481	26,929	16,675	21,266	18,440	21,277	15,364	30,770	31,543	29,323
STANDARD ERROR........DOLLARS.	124	146	166	655	219	196	195	315	207	491	615	815
MEAN NUMBER OF EARNERS...	1.79	1.94	1.99	1.83	1.68	1.26	1.00	1.00	1.00	2.13	2.15	2.10

The top row of the table also shows that about five out of six family households are married couples. Most of the remainder are families with a female householder and no husband present. Non-family households are predominantly single-person households, and women living alone outnumber men living alone.

Next look down the column for "all households" to learn the distribution of all households by income. For example, only 3,972,000 households (or 4 percent of all households), had incomes of $75,000 or more in 1985.

By looking at the cross classifications, you can discover the relative spending power of types of households. The median income row provides a quick indicator of spending power. (The median is the number in the middle of a series—as many below as above.) Median income for family households is well over twice the median for non-family households. Median income for married couples is the highest of any household type, and single females living alone have the lowest median income.

The income per household member row puts a different perspective on spending power. The highest per capita income is found among single males living alone. Single females also have a higher per capita income than married couples. The reason is simply that married-couple households have more people living in them to share the income.

From the table you can also see that fewer than half of single female householders (5,694,000) had any income from earnings in 1985. The table suggests that the income of most of the women who live alone comes largely from sources other than wages, salaries, or self-employment (the definition of money income). Many women who live alone are elderly and collect social security or some other retirement income. The table also shows that wage-earning female householders with no husband present had the lowest median earnings of any household type in 1985.

Table 6 can also answer such questions as "How many married couples in the United States in 1985 had total money income between $20,000 and $40,000?" (Answer: over 19 million.)

Even more information can be derived from the numbers by calculating percentages and using other analytic techniques, and by studying the relationships between different categories. Perhaps most important is to do what the author of the article or report did when writing the text—reflect on the meaning behind the statistics. That is their true value.

How To Evaluate Population Estimates

by William P. O'Hare

If the data you need to gauge an estimate's accuracy are available, then you don't need the estimate. Here are a few rules of thumb that can help you judge the accuracy of population estimates.

Two years before the next census and eight years since the last, just how good are those population estimates you're using?

Each year, the Census Bureau produces estimates of the total population of states and counties through its Federal-State Cooperative Program for Local Population Estimates. In this program, the bureau publishes estimates that it and the states have agreed upon. The bureau uses its county numbers to produce estimates of the population of metropolitan areas. Every two years, the bureau also produces estimates for 39,000 government units that once received General Revenue Sharing funds, including all cities, towns, villages, and subcounty jurisdictions. The revenue-sharing program has ended, but the estimates will continue.

The Census Bureau tests its estimates extensively, and the patterns observed in these tests provide a set of guidelines about the likely accuracy of population estimates in general. The most recent evaluations are published in the Census Bureau's Current Population Reports series: state estimates are evaluated in Series P-25, No. 957; county estimates are evaluated in Series P-25, No. 984; and subcounty units in Series P-25, No. 963.

Generally, these rules of thumb can also be applied to the population estimates and projections for census tracts, zip code areas, block groups, and other pieces of geography produced by private data companies.

RULE 1. Large populations can be estimated more accurately than small populations.

It is easier to estimate the population of New York City than a small village in upstate New York because random fluctuations have a much bigger impact on small populations than on large ones. Also, large cities often have better administrative records on which to base estimates.

As the size of a population increases, there is a steady decline in an estimate's error (see chart). Fifty-nine percent of places with populations of less than 100 have estimation errors in excess of 20 percent, and the average error for these places is 35 percent. But for places with populations of 100,000 or more, the average error is only 3.9 percent, and none are off by 20 percent or more. Average error for all places is 15 percent.

RULE 2. Moderately growing populations can be estimated more accurately than rapidly growing or declining populations.

The 1980 estimates for populations that had fallen by 15 percent during the 1970s had an average error of 36 percent when compared with the 1980 census results. The average error for populations that grew by 50 percent or more was 22 percent. Yet the average error for populations that grew less than 10 percent was only 10 percent.

RULE 3. Averaging several estimates of the population of an area is usually more accurate than relying on only one estimate.

The exception to this rule is when one estimation technique is far superior to others.

RULE 4. Adjusting estimates to match an independently derived control total reduces error.

Estimates of counties within a state, for example, or states within the country as a whole, improve when they are forced to sum to an independent estimate of the total area. The bureau uses this technique to produce its subcounty estimates.

RULE 5. It is easier to estimate changes over a short period of time than over a long period of time.

Most estimates begin with the decennial census population and include changes to the population since the census. There will be less error in a population estimate for 1982 than for 1987, since 1982 is closer to the benchmark year.

RULE 6. The populations for smaller places are more likely to be overestimated than the populations of larger places.

Of the 2,425 places in the U.S. with a population of 100 or less, 55 percent were overestimated, according to the 1980 census results. On the other hand, only 37 percent of the 160 places with populations of 100,000 or more were overestimated.

RULE 7. Places that lost population between 1970 and 1980 were much more likely to be overestimated than those that grew rapidly.

Fully 85 percent of the places that lost more than 15 percent of their population during the 1970s were overestimated according to the 1980 census. Only 23 percent of places that grew by more than 50 percent were overestimated.

Finally, some populations are not worth estimating. For almost half of places with fewer than 500 people, it was just as accurate in 1980 to use the 1970 census figure as the 1980 estimate. For one out of five places with populations of 100,000 or more, the 1970 census figure was a more accurate reflection of the 1980 population than was the 1980 estimate.

As with all rules, there may be some exceptions to these generalizations. Nonetheless, hard evidence about the accuracy of population estimates is seldom available, and these guidelines provide the best basis for evaluating some of the most basic demographic tools.

To paraphrase one prominent demographer, there are three standard requirements for anyone engaged in producing population estimates: one, a good database; two, a good set of assumptions; and three, a good sense of humor.

Expect larger errors when estimating smaller populations.

(percent error by population size for 1980 estimates; calculated by comparing the Census Bureau's 1980 estimates with 1980 census results)

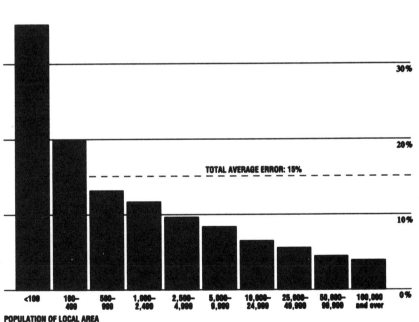

Source: U.S. Bureau of the Census, "Evaluation of 1980 Subcounty Population Estimates," Current Population Reports, Series P-25, No. 963.

HOW TO BUY SMART

YOU'VE GOT TO KNOW WHAT YOU'RE DOING when you buy cluster analysis, psychographic research, income data, wave analysis, and other aspects of demographic research. The following articles originally appeared in *American Demographics* magazine.

How to Read A Demographic Report

by James A. Paris

Understanding demographic data requires a knowledge not readily encountered in the workplace. Here are some guidelines for marketers who need to analyze neighborhood-sized areas.

When the Greek hero Theseus entered the labyrinth of Crete, he carried with him a roll of thread to unwind as he wandered through the maze in search of the Minotaur. Today's marketers need the same kind of assistance when confronted by the twistings and turnings of demographic data.

Researchers today take for granted computer access to demographic data. It was not until 1973, however, that it first became possible to retrieve data for a custom piece of geography. Now anyone can obtain demographic reports for any area in the United States—regardless of its geographic configuration.

Today, for a price ranging from $75 to $150, you can get enough demographic information to analyze any area as a possible site for a business, often within 24 hours of placing an order. If you prefer hands-on control of the data, the major demographic data companies also offer timesharing services, as well as data on computer tape or diskettes for analysis on microcomputers.

CHOOSING A STUDY AREA

Before you can start your analysis of a site, you have to make some decisions. First you have to choose your study area, then the demographic variables you want to examine for that study area. Most marketers study concentric circles around a site, or polygons, or standard political or census geography.

Concentric circles and polygons are called geometric study areas. Private data companies use the data available for standard political and census geography to approximate the data for a geometric study area.

Concentric circles, or rings, are the "quick and dirty" route in site analysis. They allow you to compare the demographics in geographically diverse areas of equal size.

But ring analysis ignores natural barriers (such as rivers or mountains) as well as areas which might fall inside a ring but have greater economic ties with areas outside the ring. Polygons are a more thoughtful way of defining a study area. The telephone companies use polygons to define their wire centers, for example, which are distinct from standard political, postal, or census boundaries. Wire centers are mutually exclusive and cover all parts of the U.S.

If you are interested in examining an irregular area, you can draw the boundaries of the area on a map and ask a demographic data company to "digitize" it. Digitizing is the process of assigning latitude and longitude coordinates for each twist and turn of the polygon that defines the area. The private data company then accumulates the census data for the parts of census geography that fall inside the polygon. Even if small-area census boundaries change with the 1990 census, the polygons you define today will still be valid ten years from now because they are coded by latitude and longitude.

FROM ADI TO ZIP

Standard geography includes postal areas (zip codes), political areas (states, counties, cities), census areas (metropolitan statistical areas, census tracts, block groups, enumeration districts), telephone areas (area codes and three-digit prefix calling areas), and media marketing areas (DMAs and ADIs).

The kind of area you choose to study depends on how much time you have, how large your budget is, and perhaps more importantly, the degree of accuracy you need for making a decision about the site. If you're submitting a construction loan application to a bank, for example, you'll need greater accuracy than if you're analyzing an area to decide whether to purchase a mailing list.

WHAT NEXT?

Once you have chosen your study area, you have to decide what data you need. Most private data companies sell a basic demographic report package consisting of one or two pages of demographic statistics. If you're buying packaged data, the report should include:
• Population in 1980, in the current year, and a five-year projection.
• Count of households in 1980, in the current year, and a five-year projection.
• Income in 1980, in the current year, and a five-year projection.
• Current distribution of households by size.
• Current average household size.
• Current size of the group quarters population.
• Current count of persons by race and Spanish origin.

• Current age/sex structure of the population (population pyramid).
• Selected 1980 housing characteristics, such as occupancy rate, owners and renters, and units per structure.

Thousands of other data items are available for marketers who have specialized needs. An Italian restaurant chain might want the count of persons of Italian ancestry, for example. An auto parts store might ask for the number of households owning two or more vehicles. And a home center may want the count of owner-occupied homes built before 1960. Most of this additional data will come from the 1980 census, but this makes it no less valuable as a tool with which to compare different sites.

Sometimes by looking at more detailed data than that provided by packaged reports, you can discover that an area is unusual and should be treated differently in your analysis. A neighborhood in which the residents are primarily Vietnamese immigrants, for example, or whose residents all live in mobile homes, is not the same as the average American community. Yet such important details frequently go by the board in a limited demographic analysis.

BENCHMARKS

You will need to order benchmark reports against which to compare your study area. Some good benchmarks are the United States as a whole, and reports for the state, metropolitan area, county, or city in which a site is located. In addition, by analyzing several areas of comparable size in the same market, or larger areas around the study area, you can glean valuable insights about a site.

To illustrate benchmarking, let's look at an imaginary Ohio community named Harrisonville. The primary study area is the three-mile radius around a site in Harrisonville; the secondary study area is the five-mile radius around the site which includes the primary study area. The benchmarks are Steele County, the State of Ohio, and the United States as a whole.

There are 20,000 data items in the 1980 census. Most of them are of interest only to federal, state, regional, county, and municipal planners. Approximately 2,000 items—about 10 percent of the total—are of any interest to marketers in the private sector. Here we look only at the eight data items most frequently requested by Urban Decision System's customers.

WHAT'S HAPPENING IN HARRISONVILLE, OHIO?

The primary study area enjoyed moderate population growth between 1970 and 1985. But the secondary study area (within the five-mile radius) lost population. The county is a big population loser, with a cumulative 15.6 percent loss since 1970; and the state as a whole has grown only slightly. Coincidentally, the population growth in the primary study area is close to the national average.

The population measured by the 1980 census is the residential population. Excluded are persons who work in the area and live elsewhere, people who are visiting the area, and people who are just passing through. In some locations, however, these groups might account for most of a store's business—a lunch stand in a city's financial district, for example, or at a service station along an interstate highway.

Some demographic data companies offer estimates of the so-called daytime population of an area based on employment statistics by industry. At this time, however, there is no reliable way to obtain anything more than a head count of an area's private-sector employees. Excluded from this count are such groups as housewives, the unemployed, students, and government employees.

THE GROUP QUARTERS

You may not think you need a count of persons in institutions and other group quarters when you're doing a site-location analysis. But in an area near a large military installation, a college, a home for the aged, a prison, or a state hospital, if you fail to consider that a large percentage of the population does not participate in the normal economy, you risk overstating the area's market potential.

In the Harrisonville primary and secondary study areas, the percent of persons in group quarters and institutions is lower than the county and state average (table 2). If the percent exceeded the national average by more than a few percentage points, it's important to find out why.

HARRISONVILLE'S HOUSEHOLDS

Households are not the same as families. A family is a household that includes a householder and one or more persons related to the householder by blood, marriage, or adoption. Non-family households are people living alone or with other people to whom they are not related.

Household growth usually exceeds population growth. This can lead to a seemingly paradoxical situation: the population in an area might be falling, but the demand for housing units may continue to rise. Compare, for example, the population growth in the secondary study area with the household growth from 1970 to 1980. The population fell by 1.7 percent, but there was a healthy 4.5 percent growth in households.

The answer lies in declining average household size. Households are increasing in number and decreasing in size because of smaller families and more people living alone (including the divorced and the elderly).

The numbers show that in the Harrisonville primary and secondary study areas, the rate of household formation is sluggish—especially in the secondary area. Household growth in the county and state are below the national average as well. While there will be demand for housing in the study area, unless the population ranks are swelled by in-migrants, the demand will be moderate.

TABLE 1: POPULATION COUNT

	primary study area*	secondary study area**	Steele County	Ohio	United States
Population 1970.........	24,606	83,243	1,721,000	10,652,000	203,212,000
Population 1980.........	27,605	81,841	1,498,000	10,798,000	226,546,000
Population 1985.........	29,008	82,306	1,451,000	10,734,000	238,288,000
Growth 1970–80	+12.2%	-1.7%	-12.9%	+1.4%	+11.5%
Growth 1980–85	+5.1%	+0.6%	-3.2%	-0.6%	+5.2%

TABLE 2: GROUP QUARTERS POPULATION

	primary study area*	secondary study area**	Steele County	Ohio	United States
Group quarters population 1985	199	664	24,000	234,000	6,048,000
Percent of total population	0.7%	0.8%	1.6%	2.2%	2.5%

TABLE 3: HOUSEHOLDS

	primary study area*	secondary study area**	Steele County	Ohio	United States
Households 1970............	8,505	29,880	554,000	3,289,000	63,450,000
Households 1980............	10,107	31,226	563,000	3,834,000	80,390,000
Households 1985............	10,835	31,995	558,000	3,921,000	87,016,000
Growth 1970–80............	+18.8%	+4.5%	+1.7%	+16.5%	+26.7%
Growth 1980–85............	+7.2%	+2.5%	-1.0%	+2.3%	+8.2%
Average household size 1970 ...	2.85	2.74	3.06	3.16	3.11
Average household size 1980 ...	2.71	2.60	2.62	2.76	2.75
Average household size 1985 ...	2.66	2.55	2.56	2.68	2.67

* 0 to 3 mile radius around site.   **0 to 5 mile radius around site, includes primary study area.

BLACKS AND HISPANICS

Within a five-mile radius around the Harrisonville site, the black population is proportionately two and one-half times greater than the national average, and the Hispanic share of the population is half the national average. But this racial distribution is not atypical for Steele County as a whole.

Be careful when you're working with racial and Hispanic data. These counts are from separate questions on the 1980 census questionnaire. Data on the white population includes the more than 45 percent of Hispanics who answered "white" as their race (about the same proportion answered "other"). Therefore, "white" does not necessarily mean non-Hispanic white. Remember, too, that persons of Spanish origin may include European Spaniards, black Cubans, and Asian Filipinos. The safest course is to treat Spanish origin as a separate category from race.

AGE AND SEX

While there are no startling differences between the age structure of the Harrisonville study area and the state and national profiles, the Steele County figures are different— the county's median age is fully two years older than that in the study area. Small differences in median age mean a lot. Together with the fact that the county is losing population, the age distribution suggests that the young are seeking their fortunes elsewhere, leaving the middle-aged and elderly behind. This does not, however, appear to be the case in the Harrisonville three-mile or five-mile ring area.

The ratio of males to females is about average, as it is in most areas where there are no large institutions or other group-quarters populations.

WHICH INCOME?

According to the definition used by the Bureau of the Census, income means money income. This is not the same as personal income, disposable income, or discretionary income—all of which are sometimes used by marketers. Money income is earnings, interest, dividends, royalties, net rental income, Social Security payments, and money from public assistance. In other words, it's all of the money people receive before they pay personal income taxes, Social Security taxes, and union dues.

Personal income, which is used by the Bureau of Economic Analysis, is money income plus certain noncash benefits. Disposable income is the income available to persons for spending or savings after taxes have been deducted. Discretionary income is the amount people have for spending after taxes and necessities are paid for. Personal income, disposable income, or discretionary income figures are not available for user-defined study areas.

Demographic data companies can show an area's income in several different ways: as aggregate income, per capita income, household income, or family income. Aggregate income is the total money income received by all persons 15 years old and over in an area, usually expressed as millions of dollars. In addition to persons living in households, the aggregate also includes the income of persons in group quarters.

TABLE 4: RACE AND SPANISH ORIGIN

	primary study area*	secondary study area**	Steele County	Ohio	United States
White 1985	74.4%	65.9%	73.1%	88.1%	81.9%
Black 1985	22.3%	30.4%	24.7%	10.6%	12.2%
Other 1985	3.3%	3.6%	2.2%	1.3%	5.9%
Spanish origin 1985	2.6%	3.5%	1.6%	1.1%	7.0%

TABLE 5: AGE BY SEX

	primary study area*	secondary study area**	Steele County	Ohio	United States
Males 1985	13,497	38,953	685,000	5,191,000	115,978,000
0 – 20	35.1%	34.9%	29.5%	33.0%	32.7%
21 – 44	40.0%	39.0%	36.9%	38.3%	39.1%
45 – 64	17.7%	17.5%	21.7%	19.4%	18.3%
65+	7.3%	8.6%	11.9%	9.4%	9.9%
Females 1985	15,060	43,353	766,000	5,542,000	122,310,000
0 – 20	31.2%	30.2%	25.4%	29.6%	29.7%
21 – 44	39.4%	37.9%	35.1%	36.7%	37.2%
45 – 64	17.3%	17.5%	22.4%	20.0%	19.1%
65+	12.2%	14.3%	17.0%	13.8%	14.0%
Median age 1985	30.4	30.5	32.4	29.9	30.0

TABLE 6: INCOME

	primary study area*	secondary study area**	Steele County	Ohio	United States
Per capita 1970	$3,232	—	—	—	—
Per capita 1980	$8,162	—	—	—	—
Per capita 1985	$11,966	$10,929	$11,631	$10,082	$10,307
Household median 1985	$24,966	$21,004	$23,226	$22,724	$22,268
Family median 1985	$32,193	$27,192	$29,066	$27,357	$26,056
1-person households 1985	26.7%	30.4%	27.3%	23.3%	23.5%

TABLE 7: HOUSING OCCUPANCY AND TENURE

	primary study area*	secondary study area **	Steele County	Ohio	United States
Housing units 1980	11,387	35,790	597,000	4,108,000	88,411,000
Owner-occupied.............	54.2%	48.8%	57.8%	63.8%	58.6%
Renter-occupied.............	34.5%	38.4%	36.7%	29.5%	32.3%
Vacant...................	11.3%	12.8%	5.6%	6.7%	9.1%

TABLE 8: UNITS PER STRUCTURE

	primary study area*	secondary study area**	Steele County	Ohio	United States
Housing units 1980	11,387	35,790	597,000	4,108,000	88,411,000
1 unit	68.0%	64.8%	57.8%	72.9%	69.7%
2 unit	6.1%	7.2%	13.5%	7.4%	6.4%
3–4 unit.................	6.2%	7.8%	5.0%	5.1%	5.3%
5+ unit	19.6%	20.3%	23.7%	14.6%	18.6%

* *0 to 3 mile radius around site.*   ***0 to 5 mile radius around site, includes primary study area.*

Per capita income is derived by dividing aggregate income by the total population. It is the average amount of money per person in an area, regardless of age or labor force status.

Researchers who use household income and family income interchangeably may be in for a shock, because household income is almost always lower than family income, often by several thousand dollars. This is because many non-family households contain students and retired persons with low incomes. Non-family households also tend to be smaller than family households and are more likely to have only one wage earner.

Note the large proportion of one-person households in the Harrisonville study area, significantly greater than the national proportion. Researchers should keep the share of households containing only one person in mind when comparing family and household income, because single-person households tend to depress household income statistics.

If a demographic report shows income for two or more years, the figures usually are expressed in current dollars, meaning the value of the dollars in that year.

The Harrisonville primary study area has a slightly higher per capita, household, and family income than any of the other areas shown. The secondary study area does not have this income edge, yet the secondary area includes the primary area. This means that households and families in the area between three and five miles from the site must have significantly lower incomes, pulling the total study area's median family income down by more than $5,000. If you are looking for a place to locate a business that depends on an affluent population for support, the area between three and five miles from the site fails the test.

WHOSE HOUSE?

A housing unit is "a house, apartment, mobile home or trailer, a group of rooms, or a single room occupied as a separate living quarter." This means that an apartment unit in a 75-unit building carries the same weight as a single-family house.

Private data companies usually do not sell current-year estimates or projections of housing units because an area's vacancy rate, which must be known in order to project housing units, cannot be predicted using demographic indicators. Determining an updated vacancy rate requires field research or contact with local authorities. Some of the factors that contribute to the vacancy rate are seasonal housing for migratory farm workers, vacation homes or cabins in resort areas, tenements closed because of strict rent control, and neighborhoods half-empty because of factory shutdowns.

Harrisonville had a higher-than-average vacancy rate in 1980. This suggests that you should do further research to determine if the vacancies are linked to adverse economic factors that could hurt the business you're thinking about siting there.

SINGLES AND MULTIPLES

If there are 1,000 single-family homes in an area and one condominium with 1,000 units, the split between single- and multiple-unit dwellings is fifty-fifty, despite the fact that the condominiums are all in one physical structure.

Some marketers mistakenly use another census tabulation called "units at address" for this kind of analysis. A street address is not the same as a structure, and addressing conventions can vary widely from community to community, or even in a single community. In an apartment complex, each unit may have a separate mailing address— or it may have a unit number and belong to the same address. As a result, you cannot determine the ratio of single- to multiple-unit dwellings using "units at address."

The Harrisonville study area does not depart much from the benchmark areas in its share of single-unit housing. Note, however, that Steele County has a larger proportion of duplexes than normal—a characteristic not shared by the study area.

PUTTING IT ALL TOGETHER

This analysis has shown that the three-mile radius around the Harrisonville site is a small pocket of relative affluence surrounded by a much less affluent area from three-to-five miles around the site. The overall Steele County market appears to be depressed, with a steady outflow of population and a stagnant or declining demand for housing.

If your business requires a large affluent population, then the Harrisonville site will not work. The 29,000 people in the three-mile area are moderately well-off, but the 53,000 people in the three-to-five mile area are not, nor is the population in the county as a whole. But for a business that knows how to exploit it, a small pocket of affluence like that found in the three-mile ring is an opportunity.

Demographic data are only part of the site location story. By themselves, demographic reports are useful as screening devices, allowing you to limit the number of potential sites and to focus your field work on fewer areas. The questions that need to be answered in the field include: What is the condition of the housing? Can an area be accessed conveniently by automobiles or public transportation? How is an area's economic growth and its infrastructure (roads, bridges, etc.)? Is there recent in-migration into the area? These questions are not easy to answer, but they are at least as important as what the demographic report reveals.

Still, if you look long and hard at the rows and columns of demographic statistics and manage to put two and two together, you can get a remarkably accurate picture that will help you develop a successful marketing plan.

CAST A CRITICAL EYE

by John Chapman

Buyers should be cautious with zip code data when accuracy is critical. And if you're targeting specific income groups be aware that there are wide variations in updated income data at the local level.

Until the 1990 census, there are no real yardsticks for evaluating the reliability of small-area estimates and projections. Yet the reliability of these numbers is vital to those who use such data in making important business investment decisions.

The International Council of Shopping Centers decided to find out how much of a difference there can be in the small area estimates and projections offered by several of the nation's private data companies. Six vendors agreed to take part in an ICSC project analyzing the variation in their numbers. The companies were CACI, Claritas, Donnelley Marketing Information Services, National Decision Systems, National Planning Data Corporation, and Urban Decision Systems.

The purpose of this project was not to determine which vendors were right or wrong. Instead, the ICSC wanted to determine how much and under what conditions small area estimates diverge. The purpose of this project was to alert the users of small area data to the importance of casting a critical eye on the numbers. Buyers should understand the methodology behind small area data, and they should verify the numbers by visiting sites before making any important business decision. Nothing in this report should be taken as an endorsement or indictment of the vendors. Since we do not have up-to-date census counts for all the geographic areas the ICSC examined, there are no objective standards for evaluating the reliability of the small area data.

SELECTING THE SITES

The ICSC examined numbers for three metropolitan areas: Baltimore, Maryland; Detroit, Michigan; and Phoenix, Arizona. The Council picked these areas because they represent a spectrum of population trends—from population loss to moderate and rapid population growth. For each metropolitan area, the ICSC requested data for four levels of geography: the metropolitan areas as a whole, a county within the metropolitan area, a group of census tracts, and a zip code approximating the census tract aggregation.

The ICSC requested from each vendor current estimates and projections of the population and number of households, current average household size, current number and percent of households within broad income groups, and average household income. The vendors supplied the numbers to the ICSC between mid-August and early September 1986.

THE DIFFERENCES

The larger the coefficient, the greater the differences among the small area estimates. The differences are the greatest for rapidly growing areas and for the smallest pieces of geography.

(coefficients of variation among vendor estimates and projections)

	BALTIMORE	DETROIT	PHOENIX*
Metropolitan Area			
Current population	0.2	0.4	2.6
Projected population	0.7	2.3	4.5
Current number of households	1.9	1.6	4.6
Projected number of households	3.9	4.0	6.2
County			
Current population	0.2	0.5	2.6
Projected population	1.2	2.7	4.5
Current number of households	1.8	1.5	4.6
Projected number of households	3.5	4.0	6.2
Zip Code			
Current population	13.2	4.4	22.1
Projected population	14.9	4.3	28.4
Current number of households	12.9	4.3	22.8
Projected number of households	14.0	5.4	28.7
Tract Aggregation			
Current population	3.5	3.7	21.5
Projected population	4.7	4.0	31.2
Current number of households	3.1	3.8	21.2
Projected number of households	4.0	5.3	30.8

* The Phoenix metropolitan area and county are the same unit of geography.

To evaluate the degree of difference among the vendors' estimates and projections, the ICSC used two statistical measures: the coefficient of variation to evaluate the estimates and projections of population and households, and Cramer's V statistic to evaluate the household income distributions.

The coefficient of variation shows the degree of difference among the companies' current estimates and five-year projections of population, and among the current estimates and five-year projections of households. The coefficient of variation is an index. When there is little divergence among the companies' numbers, the coefficient is low. As the differences increase, the coefficients rise.

At the metropolitan and county level, the degree of difference among the vendors is comparatively small. The vendor estimates and projections are most similar at the metropolitan and county level in Baltimore and Detroit—areas with relatively stable populations. All of the vendors currently estimate the Baltimore metropolitan area population at approximately 2.3 million; the coefficient of variation is 0.2 and the estimates differ by no more than 10,000. For Detroit, the current metropolitan population is estimated at 4.3 million and the vendor figures differ by no more than 40,000.

In the fast-growing Phoenix metropolitan area, the differences are greater. The vendors estimate the current population at 1.8 to 1.9 million; that is, the low and high estimates differ by about 100,000 (a coefficient of 2.6).

The differences increase in the five-year projections. There is a high degree of consensus in projecting Baltimore's metropolitan population. With a coefficient of 0.7, the vendors differ by no more than 40,000. In Detroit, on the other hand, the vendors differ by as much as 250,000 and the coefficient of variation is 2.3. The Phoenix projections differ by a similar amount but, because of the smaller base, the coefficient of variation is 4.5. Because the vendors make different assumptions about average household size, the estimated and projected numbers of households differ more among the vendors than do the population projections.

The differences among the vendors are most pronounced for the small areas of geography, particularly in Phoenix. For the Phoenix census tract aggregation, the current population estimates range from about 35,000 to roughly 62,000, with a coefficient of variation of 21.5. The coefficient of variation peaks at 31.2 for the projected population within this tract aggregation. in this case, the population projections range from 38,000 to 86,000—a difference of 48,000.

The coefficient of variation is much smaller for the Detroit and Baltimore tract aggregations. In both cases, the estimates and projections differ by no more than a few thousand and the coefficient of variation ranges from 3.1 to 5.3.

Unlike census tracts, zip codes are not standardized units of geography with field boundaries and trends updated by census data. Since businesses often use zip codes as units of analysis, however, the data vendors have developed procedures for allocating census tract information and reaggregating it on a zip code basis.

The Baltimore zip code analysis clearly illustrates the difficulties in allocating and aggregating tract information. The zip code includes five of the tracts in their entirety and parts of eight others. While the coefficients of variation among the private data companies at the tract aggregation level in Baltimore are relatively modest, they are significantly higher at the zip code level. The vendor estimates of current population for the zip code range from 26,000 to 36,000 and the coefficient of variation is 13.2. For the other variables within the Baltimore zip code, the coefficients range from 12.9 to 14.9.

HOW MANY RICH?

Unlike the population and household data, the vendor estimates of annual household income are not a single data point but a distribution among three groups: under $25,000, $25,000 to $49,999, and $50,000 and over. To determine the magnitude of the differences in the percentage income distributions from the various vendors, the ICSC used the Cramer's V statistic, which can vary from 0 to 1.0. Cramer's V approaches 1.0 as the differences among distributions increase. But for the income distributions provided by the vendors, Cramer's V never rises above 0.08, showing that the differences among the vendors in the percentage income distribution of an area's households are insignificant.

But if you use the number of households within income ranges provided by the vendors, there are substantial differences. The estimated number of households in Baltimore County with incomes of $50,000 and over, for example, ranges from 47,000 to 71,000. A business considering siting a store in Baltimore County that targets upper-income households might go ahead if it used the high set of numbers, but might abandon the idea if it used the low set.

This analysis demonstrates that there is relatively little difference in the population and household totals provided by the data companies at the metropolitan and county levels. Also, within stable market areas, the differences among the providers are not great for standard units of geography even as small as census tracts. Buyers can be confident that, regardless of the data company they use, the numbers would not be much different.

In rapidly changing areas, on the other hand, a buyer would be wise to verify small area data through field investigation and interviews with local sources such as public planning agencies.

Because of the difficulties in defining zip code geography and allocating census tract information to zip codes, buyers should be cautious with zip code data when accuracy is critical. Likewise, businesses targeting specific income groups should be aware that there are wide variations in updated income data at the local level.

HOW TO RIDE LOCAL DEMOGRAPHIC WAVES

by Dowell Meyers

Cluster analysis helps select retail sites, and demographic wave analysis can reveal the future of a market. With both tools, businesses can better anticipate the needs of their local customers.

Retailers paid little attention to demographic details before the mid-1970s, focusing instead on the overall rise or fall in population and income. The baby-boom generation changed that. The demographic roller coaster caused by the baby boom forced businesses to look beyond total population and examine the shifting age structure behind it.

This task can be hard to do in a local area because most of the available data on demographic change are national, such as the Census Bureau's Current Population Survey, but it is possible if you know the techniques.

To forecast local retail sales, retailers traditionally project the per capita income, median household income, or median family income for a market area five or ten years into the future. They then subtract federal, state, and local taxes and contributions to pensions or insurance, multiplying the result by the number of people, households, or families in an area. The result is a rough estimate of the total income available for consumer purchases.

In increasingly competitive markets, this approach is not enough. It ignores the changing age structure and household composition of an area, and it glosses over the critical lifestyle changes that affect consumer behavior. There are two ways to get at these factors locally—with geodemographic clusters, and with census data.

THE CLUSTERS

Cluster analysis categorizes neighborhoods by lumping together such characteristics as income, age, housing type, education, and occupation. It assumes that averages describe the consumers in a neighborhood. In reality, no neighborhood is made up of residents who are all the same, although averages are a useful way to compare neighborhoods.

But cluster statistics can now be compared with the results of national consumer surveys from companies like Mediamark Research, Simmons Market Research Bureau, and National Panel Diary. The survey data show the consumer behavior of different demographic groups. For example, higher-income households buy more imported cheeses than those with lower incomes, and the brands they buy vary by the educational level of the householder.

Linking survey data with geodemographic clusters is a matter of classifying survey respondents according to their neighborhood cluster type. If the respondents adequately represent cluster types, a simple calculation shows the proportion of residents in each cluster who could be expected to buy imported cheeses from a local retail store.

The next step in this type of analysis is to construct an index of sales potential for imported cheese for each cluster type. An index of 150, for example, indicates that a particular cluster has a sales potential for imported cheese that is 50 percent greater than the average for all clusters. By assigning an index of sales potential to each cluster within a market and weighting it according to the proportions of the market represented by each cluster, businesses can pinpoint the hottest markets among dozens of possibilities.

THE WAVES

A second way to analyze a local market is to see how it changes over time. By analyzing local demographic waves, businesses can plot changes in the local age structure and predict shifts in the demand for products and services at the local level.

The age profile of the residents of census tracts, each of which contain approximately 4,000 people, can change significantly during a decade. By examining the changes in the tracts in a local market, retailers can predict future changes and plan accordingly.

By plotting the age profile of a tract's population in 1970 and 1980 on a graph, retailers can see the changes in the tract's age distribution. The changes are caused by births, deaths, and migration as well as the aging of the population.

The combination of an aging population and migration causes demographic "waves" to move in time within census tracts. Household size can drop sharply in an area of older homes as children grow up and move away. But if younger families move into these neighborhoods and gradually replace the older residents, household size may climb again.

Local demographic waves have hit many suburbs built during the 1950s and 1960s. While the characteristics of the renters in the suburbs have not changed over the past few decades, the characteristics of homeowners have changed dramatically.

In Madison, Wisconsin, for example, neighborhoods dominated by homeowners have a high proportion of long-term residents living in older housing. In housing built

SURF'S UP

Two age peaks in 1970 became three age peaks by 1980.

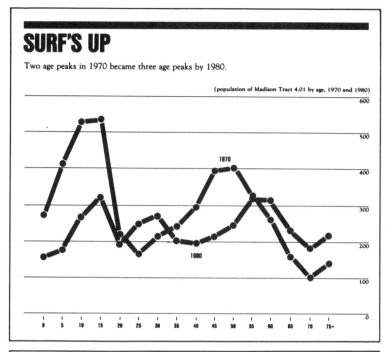

(population of Madison Tract 4.01 by age, 1970 and 1980)

TIDE'S OUT

Projections show new age peaks at 35 and 75+ in 1990, and 45 and 75+ in 2000.

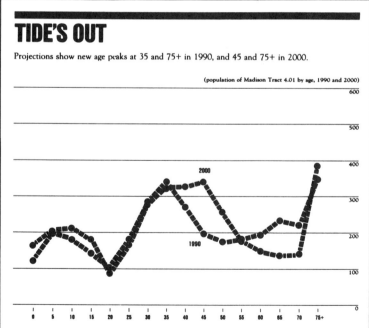

(population of Madison Tract 4.01 by age, 1990 and 2000)

between 1940 and 1959, nearly 60 percent of the residents have lived there ten or more years. Thirty-six percent have lived there at least 20 years. In contrast, 90 percent of the renters living in housing built between 1940 and 1959 have lived there less than ten years.

The 1970 age profile for Madison Tract 4.01 shows two population peaks—at ages 10 to 15 and 45 to 50. In 1980, this tract had three smaller peaks at ages 15, 25 to 30, and 55 to 60. Fewer children live in the tract in 1980 than did in 1970 because the 1970s were baby-bust years, and because of the departure of children from their families' homes.

More adults in their 20s live in the tract in 1980 than did in 1970 as the age 15 peak of 1970 grew up. And the 1980 peak at ages 55 to 60 indicates that residents are aging in place—the 45-to-50-year-olds of 1970 have continued to live in the tract. In fact, young families have difficulty moving into the area because older homeowners are staying put.

Once you plot the tract's changes between 1970 and 1980, the next step is to project what will happen to the tract in the future. To do this you have to make assumptions about birth rates, death rates, and net migration. I used one set of assumptions on Tract 4.01 and generated age profiles for 1990 and 2000 with a personal computer spreadsheet program.

The population projection for Tract 4.01 shows that the age 25 peak of 1980 is age 35 in 1990 and age 45 in 2000. The number of residents aged 75 and older grows rapidly as the middle-aged residents of 1970 move into retirement.

THE MARKET EFFECTS

To assess the impacts of local demographic change, businesses need to keep several factors in mind.

First, the demographic waves of the 1960s and 1970s should moderate in the 1980s and 1990s. But the aging baby-boom generation will still dominate local markets.

Second, local demographic waves can make income measures—especially per capita income—a misleading indicator of purchasing power. The per capita of a neighborhood with a high proportion of children will underestimate the purchasing power of householders. But per capita income in a neighborhood dominated by middle-aged householders may overestimate purchasing power if the older householders are using money for college tuition, retirement savings, or travel instead of local purchases.

Third, consumer expenditures for basic household goods rise with age to a peak in middle age, then level off and decline. According to the Bureau of Labor Statistics' Consumer Expenditure Survey, expenditures on car parts, housekeeping supplies, personal care products, and food peak for households headed by 35-to-54-year-olds.

Local businesses that combine age-specific spending patterns with profiles of local demographic waves can see opportunities and try to fill the gaps.

Cluster analysis helps select retail sites, and demographic wave analysis can reveal the future of a market. With both tools, businesses can better anticipate the needs of their local customers.

PSYCHOGRAPHIC GLITTER AND GOLD

by Bickley Townsend

There's gold in lifestyle research, but it's not a get-rich-quick proposition. You still have to mine it, and that takes staying attuned to changes in the consumer marketplace.

Anheuser-Busch decided to develop a new kind of beer, one that would capitalize on the shift in consumer values toward natural products and healthy lifestyles. Given Americans' interest in diet, health, and nutrition, what could be more logical than a beer called Natural Light? But Natural Light bombed. So did Real cigarettes, positioned on a similar premise: that there are smokers who are seeking a natural, unadulterated cigarette. Anheuser-Busch eventually came up with a winner, Bud Light, but only after relinquishing the brand name and the positioning that assumed naturalness was meaningful to beer drinkers.

Psychographic segmentation promises a lot, but doesn't always deliver. Anheuser-Busch and the makers of Real cigarettes found out the hard way the danger in taking lifestyle research too far or too literally. "In both instances, the lifestyle assumptions were wrong," says Tony Adams, marketing director of Campbell Soup Company. "Attitudinal segments that may have worked in other product categories could not translate to beer and cigarettes."

But General Foods made psychographic analysis work for Sanka, which suffered from a staid, older image; after all, wasn't it only elderly people who needed decaffeinated coffee? Yet the same trend that set Anheuser-Busch off in the wrong direction—consumers' growing health-consciousness—gave General Foods the opening it needed to shift Sanka's positioning. The new campaign targeted active achievers of all ages, picturing them in pursuit of adventurous lifestyles—such as running the rapids in a kayak—with the tag line that Sanka "Lets you be your best"— a classic achiever appeal.

DISSECTING PSYCHOGRAPHICS

Psychographics describes "the entire constellation of a person's attitudes, beliefs, opinions, hopes, fears, prejudices, needs, desires, and aspirations that, taken together, govern how one behaves," and that in turn, "finds holistic expression in a lifestyle" (Arnold Mitchell, The Nine American Lifestyles, New York: Macmillan, 1983, p. vii). The idea is to go beyond standard demographics to learn your best customers' dreams, hopes, fears, and beliefs. By grouping people into homogeneous segments based on their lifestyles, many marketers believe they have a new tool for understanding the consumer and increasing their bottom-line results.

"It's not to say that demographics don't matter. Of course they do," says Gene Cooper, manager of primary research at ABC News and Sports. "But it is psychological motivation which is the driving force behind behavior."

Interest in psychographics has been on the rise since marketers first began to see the mass defection of the baby-boom generation from expected patterns of behavior and consumption, as the children of Buick-driving Republicans registered Democratic and bought Volkswagens. Even pizza caught on big, according to some observers, because it was the perfect protest food: not only did parents not like it at first, but eating it violated one of the basic rules the boomers had grown up with—never eat with your fingers.

DO-IT-YOURSELF PSYCHOGRAPHICS

Researchers who want information on values and lifestyles can buy Yankelovich Clancy Shulman's Monitor, subscribe to VALS (see page 196 for more details about the Monitor and VALS), or they can develop their own psychographic segmentation system. Sometimes the choice is determined by cost or convenience. How appropriate an "off-the-shelf" system may be, compared with a tailored segmentation study, also affects the choice.

When ABC wanted to segment the television-viewing audience, it considered using VALS, but rejected it as not applicable enough to its needs. Moreover, says ABC's Cooper, "We believe that many of the VALS groups are demographically driven." So ABC developed its own system for classifying viewers into clusters relevant to television viewing. ABC interviewed a national probability sample of 1,000 respondents by telephone, using an 81-item questionnaire designed to measure self-esteem, opinion leadership, need for group inclusion, cosmopolitanism, and other psychological attributes. Cooper emphasizes that, "First, we did not use demographics to form the groups. Second, we did not use any television viewing or program-preference items in the cluster instrument. Our approach was to use fundamental psychological attributes which we felt would be far more stable and more powerful than transient items related to television."

A factor analysis resulted in eight cluster groups in three broad categories: a "mainstream middle-America" group, a group that is out of the mainstream in various ways, and a "counter-mainstream" group. Individual clusters were given names like Organized Participants, Family Oriented, Liberal Cosmopolitan, and Rigid and Resistant.*

ABC continues to expand the role of psychographics in its research efforts—for program diagnostics, scheduling, and promotion, and in examining potential markets for new technologies such as pay-cable services.

PROMISE OR PERFORMANCE

Has the performance of psychographic segmentation met its promise? It depends on who you talk to. Some researchers question the methodology. "VALS is the Reader's Digest of marketing research," says Edward Spar, president of Market Statistics. "With these predigested, prepackaged systems, someone else gives you the answers and as a statistician, that makes me a little nervous. They won't tell you the factor loadings or rotations or the explained variance."

John Mather, senior vice president and director of marketing research in Ketchum Advertising's Pittsburgh office, doesn't have any problem with VALS' proprietary secrets. "That's the little black box—it's how they keep us. I know from my own graduate work that a discriminant-function model takes a lot of time to build and refine to be sure it's valid and reliable." Adds Francois Christen, a VALS manager, "The proof is in the pudding—whether VALS predicts how people will differ in terms of product consumption and use. Clearly, it does."

Other critics question how useful psychographic research is, arguing that too often it tells you what you already know. "One of the most frustrating aftermaths of any research is a result that is so obvious everyone is thinking 'So what's new?'" says Tony Adams of Campbell Soup.

Cluster analysis is often described as lifestyle analysis, but this is a misconception reinforced by cluster names like Porch Swings & Apple Pie, Blue Blood Estates, and Tough Times.

The four cluster systems (CACI's ACORN, Claritas' PRIZM, Donnelley Marketing's ClusterPlus, and National Decision System's VISION) are based not on attitudes or values, but on demographic data. They can complement psychographics by helping to locate the target segments "on the ground," while psychographics tell you how to shape the message.

Think about a bag lady living in a low-rent hotel room, Adams asks. "Do we need a battery of lifestyle questions to label this consumer as a light user of Gucci shoes, Jordache jeans, Chivas Regal, and Godiva chocolates?" It doesn't help, he adds, when researchers attempt to dress up the obvious: "Men and women who like to cook become Culinary Artisans; people involved in church and community become the Societally Conscious." Why not use plain English instead of jargon, asks Adams.

Psychographic researchers acknowledge that most people don't fit a pure type. In the VALS system, all respondents are assigned a score not only for their primary lifestyle type, but also for each of the other VALS types, based on how closely their questionnaire responses conform to the profile of each type. The VALS researchers have gone further by specifying important subgroups within lifestyle segments. For example, if your customers are primarily Achievers, they might be Achiever/Belongers, Achiever/Societally Conscious, or Super Achievers. Although each group scores highest in the Achiever segment, there are important differences. While Achiever/Belongers are relatively conservative, older, female, and less well-educated, Achiever/Societally Conscious people are more apt to be younger professionals, socially liberal, and able to say "I've got all I need; now I'm ready to start contributing to causes and getting involved in the community," as Ketchum Advertising's John Mather explains it. Super Achievers, by contrast, are "win at all costs" workaholics, totally committed to success in their fields, the most male, most managerial, most affluent, and most Republican of any Achiever subgroup.

Where your customers cluster among these Achiever subgroups may make a difference in how you pitch your product. Such cross-classification is an attempt to increase the subtlety of the VALS typology, although, says Mather, "a lot of us are still trying to become better users of the primary groupings."

GOLD IN THE GLITTER

There's gold in the psychographic glitter, but it's not a get-rich-quick proposition. You still have to mine it, and that takes staying attuned to changes in the consumer marketplace. America is moving into the "decade of the real thing," according to VALS' Arnold Mitchell, celebrating light food and drink, natural products and processes, having a "love affair with the lemon," as Ann Clurman, director of Yankelovich Clancy Shulman's Monitor, has quipped. These are useful insights into lifestyle trends—but they didn't work for Real cigarettes or Natural Light beer.

"It's important to remember," cautions Ketchum's John Mather, "that lifestyle analysis is not a panacea, it's not the magic crystal ball we've all been looking for in our file cabinets. But used well, psychographics can give us that critical bit of insight we need for added leverage in the marketplace."

TIPS FOR FINDING THE INFORMATION YOU NEED

by Diane Crispell

WHEN LOOKING FOR INFORMATION, YOU SHOULD consider several things before you start—subject, geographic level, time period, services, timeliness, cost, and quality of information.

1. SUBJECT

You can get just about anything from the Census Bureau, from general population characteristics to consumer expenditures to retail sales. The kind of data available from other federal agencies is usually obvious from the name; e.g., National Center for Health Statistics, Bureau of Labor Statistics, etc.

The state and local sources have population data, some economic information, and vital statistics (births, deaths, marriages, and divorces), but not consumer data.

The private data companies are listed by the general type of service they provide—demographic data, mapping, forecasting, etc. Most offer a combination of population and consumer data.

2. GEOGRAPHIC LEVEL

In general, federal agencies have national data only. The exception is the Bureau of the Census, which has detailed data for census-defined areas (regions, states, counties, MSAs, census tracts, minor civil divisions, etc.) for 1980 only, and annual industry data for states and counties. The Bureau of Labor Statistics has limited state and metropolitan area information, and the Bureau of Economic Analysis also has some small area data.

State and local sources usually have data for the state, counties, metropolitan areas, and sometimes for cities and towns.

Private data companies are the wizards of geography. Several produce data for virtually any geographic area—zip codes, polygons, census tracts—although others have national survey data only.

Nonprofit organizations vary a great deal in their geographic coverage as well as in their data availability and services.

3. TIME PERIOD

All data are not available for all time periods. Projections are especially limited. Historic data may not exist if a characteristic was not significant in the past; they may also not be comparable with current definitions. How current your data have to be is often a question of priority—for some people, 1980 census data are recent enough, for others 1988 information is essential.

The private data companies are the most up-to-date. Many do annual updates of their population estimates for any geographic area. However, their forecasts are usually short-term (five-year); only a few project as far as the year 2000, and this is usually at the national level only. In many cases, the federal government has the most extensive projections for the country as a whole.

Some data are collected and updated regularly; others are one-time only. Many market studies fall into the latter category, as do some federal surveys. When you are looking for information, don't be surprised to find that it was last gathered in 1978.

4. SERVICES

The form that information comes in ranges from tables of statistics to market studies of consumer trends to microcomputer software to thematic maps. Government data are mostly in the form of volumes of numerical tables and computer tapes. Private data companies provide much of their information in almost any medium.

Both government and private sources may do customized data analysis (such as a special cross-tabulation of census data). The trade-off is between timeliness and cost. Private firms will do the work quickly, but may cost more; a government agency may have a lower price, but a longer turnaround time. The computer capability of sources varies. Many state and local sources can do custom analysis of government data tapes; they usually have national data as well as those for their own state.

5. TIMELINESS

Timeliness is not an issue for private data companies. As soon as they update their estimates and projections, or conduct their surveys, they are ready to go. Some firms provide same-day turnaround even on customized data reports. This is not the case for most federal agencies and state and local sources. It can take literally years to get published results of government data. You can often phone to get unpublished information, but even this may take awhile, because agencies are not funded or staffed sufficiently for immediate data analysis.

6. COST

If you have to consider cost when you are looking for information (as most of us do), you may decide to take older government data for free rather than current proprietary estimates for what can be a hefty fee. The general rule is that government data are older but much cheaper. Information from nonprofit organizations may be free or inexpensive, but not always. Data from private data companies can range from an inexpensive printed report to a costly series of reports.

7. QUALITY OF INFORMATION

Although it is beyond the scope of this guide to provide a methodological review of data sources, suffice it to say that data quality varies a great deal. In general, government data are the best around—the most accurate and least biased. Other sources vary as to their method of data collection, estimation and projection procedures, and analysis. We recommend shopping around and talking to sources about how they obtain their information.

FEDERAL AGENCIES

GENERALLY SPEAKING, FEDERAL AGENCIES ONLY have national data; that is, they usually do not have data for states, counties, and so on. The only exceptions are the Bureau of the Census and the Bureau of Economic Analysis.

Furthermore, data from federal agencies often take a long time to compile and an even longer time to publish, so they may not be current. Projections are available from various agencies, but again, they are usually national in coverage. The advantage of these data is that they are collected by the government and are probably the most accurate. They are also relatively inexpensive.

An important note: the government has more data than most people realize; take advantage of it.

U.S. BUREAU OF THE CENSUS

Data User Services Division
Washington, D.C. 20233
301-763-4100

The U.S. Census Bureau is by far the world's largest supplier of demographic data. It counts everybody in the United States once every ten years with the census, and it monitors ongoing changes with the monthly Current Population Survey and the Survey of Income and Program Participation.

The Bureau also conducts many surveys for other branches of the government, and has an enormous network of specialists in population, housing, economic, and geographic areas. Ordering information is at the end of this section.

CONTACT

Customer Services
301-763-4100

(See page 101 for a complete list, by subject, of the phone numbers of the hundreds of specialists who can answer your questions about everything from aging population to county business patterns.)

FOR MORE INFORMATION

A very useful publication for understanding everything the Census Bureau offers and how to order it is the annual *Census Catalog and Guide,* available from the Superintendent of Documents, Government Printing Office, Washington, DC 20402; phone 202-783-3238. It's about $21, and you can pay with MasterCard or Visa. You can also call the friendly and helpful Customer Services staff at the Census Bureau: 301-763-4100.

WHAT YOU CAN GET FROM THE CENSUS BUREAU

Current Population Survey (CPS)

You can get up-to-date estimates and projections of population size and characteristics from the Current Population Survey.

Each month, CPS interviewers ask people in about 60,000 households across the country about their employment-related activities during the preceding week. Each household is interviewed for four consecutive months, dropped for eight months, and then interviewed over the same four months the following year.

Computer tapes

Tapes from the regular part of the survey, which gathers data for the Department of Labor's monthly report on employment and unemployment, are usually available within two months of the survey.

Tapes for supplementary questions to the survey, which gather the data for the Current Population Reports, are usually not ready until at least six months after the survey. Order from Customer Services at the Census Bureau.

Printed Reports Also Available

The bureau issues four series of CPS reports:

Population Characteristics (series P-20)

The annual reports are on education, fertility, geographic residence and mobility, households and families, marital status, Spanish origin, etc.; biennial reports examine voter registration and participation.

Size and Characteristics of the Farm Population (series P-27)

These reports examine the U.S. farm population by age, sex, race, Spanish origin, marital status, fertility, employment status, poverty status, family income, metropolitan-nonmetropolitan residence and employment status, etc.

Consumer Income (series P-60)

This series has tables which cross-classify income with U.S. data on race and Spanish origin, age, farm versus nonfarm residence, sex, education, occupation, marital status, size and type of family.

Special Census Bureau Studies (series P-23)

These reports furnish information about such topics as blacks, youth, women, metropolitan and non-metropolitan residents, etc. For a complete list of the almost 40 P-23 reports that are available, see the *Census Catalog and Guide*.

How to Order Printed CPS Reports

A subscription to the four series of reports is $47 a year and can be ordered from the Superintendent of Documents, Government Printing Office, Washington, DC 20402.

Estimates and Projections (series P-25)

The Census Bureau regularly provides current estimates of the population, which also contain the bureau's projections of the future U.S. population. The P-25 series includes estimates of
• total U.S. population (monthly)
• population by age, sex, and race (annual midyear)
• population of states by age (annual)
• population of counties and metropolitan areas (every two years).

The series also includes long-range projections of the population by age, race, and sex. The latest volume in the series is 1983 to 2080, and it includes data by single years of age; a report projecting the voting-age population appears in alternate years before each Congressional election. A subscription to series P-25 costs $18 a year and can be ordered from the Superintendent of Documents.

Survey of Income and Program Participation (SIPP)

SIPP, a longitudinal survey whereby a sample of households are interviewed at four-month intervals for 2-1/2 years, provides valuable data on every member of the household on labor force participation, hours and weeks the employed worked and how much they earned, why the unemployed didn't work, how much time they spent looking for work, whether and how much unemployment compensation they received. Questions cover more than 50 types of income including transfer payments, pensions and investment income; several measures of income and wealth are reported.

Order in "Waves"

SIPP computer tapes are available on a "wave-by-wave" basis, meaning that the four months of a given round of interviews are on one tape. These files are suitable for cross-sectional quarterly analysis, and researchers can also create longitudinal files by matching two or more waves. Tapes can be ordered from Customer Services at the Census Bureau.

Printed SIPP Reports Also Available

The Census Bureau provides the SIPP data in quarterly and annual cross-sectional reports. Core information reports provide a wide variety of data on labor force activity, types and amounts of income, participation in cash and noncash benefit programs, jobs held or businesses/farms owned, number of hours and weeks worked, earnings, weeks without a job or business, whether or not they were seeking employment, education, public or subsidized-rental housing, low-income energy assistance, and school breakfast and lunch participation. The SIPP written reports are $9 for an annual subscription, or $2.25 to $3.75 for a single report, and can be ordered from the Superintendent of Documents.

For More Information About SIPP
Order *Survey of Income and Program Participation Users' Guide*, which contains general information on the background, survey content, sample design, and procedures for estimation and calculation of sampling variability, as well as a glossary of selected terms; $10 from Customer Services at the Census Bureau.

Outline and Display Maps

Maps are usually published as part of the corresponding report series. But a number of separate maps are available, and in some cases it is impossible to make sense of the data without them. They generally show boundaries as of January 1, 1980, and they fall into three categories: outline maps in the publications, outline maps sold separately, and display maps.

Outline Maps in the Publications

These maps show only the areas to which data can be related, and do not show any data themselves. They cover:
• Congressional Districts
• County Subdivisions
• MSA Blocks
• State Blocks
• State CSA/MSAs
• U.S. CSA/MSAs
• Urbanized Areas

Outline Maps Sold Separately

Five basic types of outline maps are available:
• County
• Indian Reservation

- Place
- Place-and-Vicinity
- Metropolitan/Vicinity

Display Maps

These boundary outline maps sometimes include demographic or economic data. They are described in detail in the *Census Catalog and Guide*.

How to Order Maps
To order maps, or for more information, contact the Data Preparation Division, Geography Branch, Bureau of the Census, Jeffersonville, IN 47132; 812-288-3213.

OTHER PRODUCTS FROM THE CENSUS BUREAU

Because the 1980 census is so far behind us, there are many reports available from it that we feel are too outdated to be of much use. However, most of these reports will be reissued after the 1990 census, and here, briefly, is what they will contain:

Summary Tape Files (STFs)

These computer tapes, organized according to subject and geography, are summaries of census data and they contain a broad range of population and housing data from the short census questionnaire that all Americans answered and from the long form that a sample of Americans filled out.

There are five files available for use by the public from the 1980 census, and they include STF-3, the most popular file, which provides answers from the long census questionnaire to such questions as income and income type, residence in 1975, and transportation to work. STF-1 contains data collected on the short census form, while STFs 2 and 4 show detail by race and Spanish origin. STF-5, the biggest file, provides highly detailed tabulations and cross-classifications of subjects like marital history or language spoken at home. The geographies covered vary with each STF.

Public Use Microdata Sample Tapes (PUMS)

Researchers who want access to individual replies to census questionnaires use the PUMS tapes, which provide data in 5, 1, and 0.1 percent samples from the long census form. Because the Census Bureau has promised to protect the anonymity of all respondents, the PUMS files are only available for large geographic areas.

Equal Employment Opportunity (EEO) Special File

This file is based on information from the sample questionnaire and is particularly valuable for anyone who needs data for personnel recruitment and affirmative action program planning. The EEO File is based on data from the long questionnaire and has detailed occupational breakdowns and years of school completed, by age, shown by sex and Hispanic origin or race for non-Hispanics.

Printed Census Reports

The printed reports were prepared from the computer tapes and contain less data. Volume 1 of the final population reports is called "Characteristics of the Population," and it is divided into four sections or chapters:
• Chapter A. Number of Inhabitants—final population counts for a variety of geographies ranging from states to MSAs.
• Chapter B. General Population Characteristics—data on household relationship, age, race, Spanish origin, sex, and marital status for areas ranging from states to Alaska Native villages.
• Chapter C. General Social and Economic Characteristics—shows more detailed data than the Chapter B reports, and includes information from the long form on such topics as income, education, ancestry, fertility, family composition, marital history, and occupation; covers the same geographic areas as Chapter B.
• Chapter D. Detailed Population Characteristics—detailed statistics on population characteristics, cross-classified by age, race, Spanish origin, etc.

Volume 2 consists of reports on such topics as gross migration for counties, ancestry of the population by city, characteristics of the journey to work, and household and median income.

General Housing Characteristics

This series of reports parallels the population reports, and the five volumes cover:
Volume 1. Housing
Volume 2. Long form detailed housing characteristics
Volume 3. Metropolitan housing characteristics
Volume 4. Components of inventory change
Volume 5. Residential finance

Immigration Data   The 1980 census asked a sample of the population several questions that provide a snapshot of the nation's immigrants, and the resulting data are contained on computer tape and in printed reports. Information on the country of birth and year of immigration is also available on the Public Use Microdata Sample (PUMS).

HOW TO ORDER FROM THE CENSUS BUREAU
Virtually everything should be ordered directly from the Census Bureau or the Superintendent of Documents.

Ordering Data Files   Most computer tapes cost $175 per reel and are available at 1600 or 6250 bpi, EBCDIC or ASCII. All data files should be ordered from:
Data User Services Division
Customer Services
Bureau of the Census
Washington, DC 20233
301-763-4100

Ordering Publications   Unless otherwise noted, most publications are ordered from:
Superintendent of Documents
Government Printing Office
Washington, DC 20402-9325
202-783-3238

Ordering Microfiche and Microfiche Paperprints   Contact the Superintendent of Documents and Customer Services at the Census Bureau.

Product Availability & Distribution   Contact the Data User Services Division at the Census Bureau. For information on content, contact the appropriate Census Bureau specialists (see page 101).

Prices   Call the Superintendent of Documents or Customer Services at the Census Bureau.

Payment   Pay with check, money order, MasterCard, or Visa when ordering. You can also set up a pre-paid account at the Bureau and with the Superintendent of Documents.

AGRICULTURE, Department of

1301 New York
Avenue, NW
Washington, DC 20005
(See page 107 for
Subject Specialists.)

There are three groups in the Department of Agriculture that are of interest to marketers: the Population Group, which provides information about the population of farms, rural areas, and small towns; the Family Economics Research Group, which studies families nationwide, not just those that live on farms or in rural areas; and the Consumer Nutrition Center, which conducts the Nationwide Food Consumption Survey to see whether the nutritional needs of the population are being met. Each of these groups provides a wealth of data on their respective areas.

CONTACT
Ben Blankenship
202-786-1504

FOR MORE INFORMATION

• *Handbook of Agricultural Charts*, available from the Superintendent of Documents, Government Printing Office, Washington, DC 20402; price varies each year.

• *Agricultural Statistics*, also available from the Superintendent of Documents; price varies.

• *Economic Research Service (ERS) Reports*, which list new publications from the Agricultural and Rural Economics Division. To get on the free mailing list, write to the Information Division, Economic Research Service, 1301 New York Avenue, NW, Washington, DC 20250.

WHAT YOU CAN GET FROM THE DEPARTMENT OF AGRICULTURE

Continuing Survey of Food Intake by Individuals

Conducted in 1985-86, this is a dietary study of men and women aged 19 to 50 and their children under age 5. It is available from the Superintendent of Documents.

Family Economics Review

The quarterly journal of the Family Economics Research Group covers factors that affect the decisions people make about life's big events—getting married, having children, buying a house, deciding to retire. It also reports on such topics as how much it costs to raise a child, and household savings and credit use. An annual subscription is $5, single issues are $2, and it can be ordered from the Superintendent of Documents.

Hired Farm Working Force	An annual report profiling farm workers—who they are, where and when they work, and what kind of work they do.
National Food Review	The quarterly journal of the Economic Research Services covers economic issues of the food industry, not including farm production. There is also an annual issue on food consumption, expenditures, and prices. Available from the Superintendent of Documents for $5.50 a year.
Nationwide Food Consumption Survey	A periodically-conducted survey that examines foods commonly eaten by individuals, the amount per day and per eating occasion. Reports on regions are available, and data from the 1987-88 survey will be available from the Superintendent of Documents in 1989.
Size and Characteristics of the Farm Population	Series P-27 of the Current Population Reports, this annual survey from the Census Bureau identifies people who live on farms, whether or not they are farmers. It's a joint publication of the Census Bureau and the USDA, and can be ordered from the Superintendent of Documents; it is part of a series of four Current Population Reports, and you receive all of them for the annual subscription price of $47.
Other Reports Available	The Consumer Nutrition Center uses the information it gathers to estimate how much it should cost to eat at home each month for families of different sizes and individuals of different ages. These estimates are based on four food plans the center staff has made, depending on the household's income level. For prices and ordering information write to: Human Nutrition Information Service, Federal Building, Hyattsville, MD 20782.

ECONOMIC ANALYSIS, Bureau of

U.S. Department of
Commerce
1401 K Street, NW
Washington, DC 20230

The Bureau of Economic Analysis provides the only ongoing annual measure of economic activity at the regional and local levels. It examines principal sources of personal income, including transfer payments and rental income, dividend and interest income, wages, salaries, and the industries that supply them.

BEA data differ from those of the Census Bureau in that the Census Bureau, using a narrower concept of income, surveys people to learn their income and then averages the responses, while the BEA first determines the total personal income of a county or state and then divides it by the population.

CONTACT
Larry Moran
202-523-0777
(See page 108 for
Subject Specialists.)

FOR MORE INFORMATION
User's Guide to BEA Information; available for free from the BEA Public Information Office.

WHAT YOU CAN GET FROM THE BEA

Survey of Current Business

This monthly publication provides four valuable series of income data:
1. Quarterly estimates of personal income for states, which appear in the January, April, July, October issues.
2. Preliminary annual estimates of personal income for states appear in the April issue; revised estimates appear in August.
3. Annual estimates of per capita disposable personal income for states are in the August issue.
4. Estimates of personal income for counties for two years earlier appear in the April issue.

The *Survey of Current Business* is $18 from the Superintendent of Documents, Government Printing Office, Washington, DC 20402.

Local Area Personal Income

An annual publication that provides detailed income data and tabulations for the six most recent years for many geographic regions:
• Volume 1. Data for the U.S., regions, states, MSAs
• Volumes 2-8. County data and maps for the eight BEA

geographic regions (New England, Mideast, Great Lakes, Plains, Southeast, Southwest, Rocky Mountain, and Far West).

These volumes, which come out every July, vary in price and can be ordered from the Superintendent of Documents.

BEA Regional Projections

Published every five years, it provides demographic and economic projections for regions, states, and MSAs by:
1. Three age groups: 0-14, 15-64, and 65 and over
2. Personal income by source
3. Employment and earnings for 57 industrial sectors.

The seven volumes in this set are for sale by the Superintendent of Documents; an order form is available from the Regional Economic Analysis Division, Projections Branch, 1401 K Street, NW, Washington, DC 20230, or from the Superintendent of Documents. The 2-reel set of computer tapes is available from the BEA at $125 a reel. To order contact Elizabeth Rozycki at the BEA at 202-523-0936.

Tabulations

Tabulations can be requested for counties or combinations of counties and can be ordered on magnetic tape, microfiche, or computer printout. For this service, which the BEA provides relatively quickly, telephone 202-523-0966.

Data About a Particular State

State and local economic information can be had by joining a BEA user group. The user groups are listed for each of the states under the heading "State & Local Economic Information," in the chapter beginning on page 113.

EDUCATION STATISTICS, Center for

Education Information Branch
U.S. Dept. of Education
555 NJ Ave., NW
Washington, DC 20208

The primary source of data about education demographics and the American educational system, the center conducts surveys in four areas:

1. Preprimary, elementary, and secondary education
2. Colleges and universities
3. Adult and vocational education
4. A miscellaneous group that includes surveys of libraries and public television and a national longitudinal study of high school students.

CONTACTS
Fred Beamer
800-424-1616
Metro Washington area
800-626-9854
(See page 108 for Subject Specialists.)

FOR MORE INFORMATION
Catalogue of Publications lists the wide range of statistical reports that are available, many of them free. Write: Education Information Office, Center for Education Statistics, Department of Education, Washington, DC 20208; 800-424-1616 or 202-626-9854; in Washington call 800-626-9854.

WHAT YOU CAN GET FROM THE CENTER FOR EDUCATION STATISTICS

Current Population Survey

Every three years, the Census Bureau asks the people included in its May Current Population Survey about their participation in adult education and gives the center the results for analysis. The October Current Population Survey collects data on the demographic characteristics of all students. Available from the Superintendent of Documents.

Digest of Education Statistics

This annual publication contains a representative selection of education statistics gathered from the center's own surveys and a variety of other sources. Available from the Superintendent of Documents, Government Printing Office, Washington, DC 20402.

High School and Beyond

This longitudinal survey consists of biennial follow-ups of people who were high school seniors or sophomores in 1980. A report from this survey, "Four Years After High

School: A Capsule Description of 1980 Seniors," was released in 1985 and is available from the Superintendent of Documents. The 1986 report came out in 1988.

Higher Education General Information Survey

The center conducts an annual census of each college and university to gather data on enrollment, faculty, faculty salaries and tenure, degrees conferred, finances, and student charges. Annual reports and data tapes are available from the Center For Education Statistics.

Projections of Education Statistics

Every other year, the center issues ten-year projections of enrollments, graduates, teachers, and expenditures for elementary, secondary, and higher education. Projections were most recently released in the spring of 1988.

Targeted Forecasts

The center's Projections Division also issues five-year projections of key education statistics and highlights projected data for the coming term. The reports are published approximately ten times a year, and are available from the Education Information Branch at no charge.

Computer Reports and Other Services

The center gives people access to more detailed data than its publications contain via computer tape, computer printouts, and microfiche.

It also does special tabulations, although it advises anyone wanting extensive analysis to buy the tapes and do it themselves.

Finally, the Education Information Branch produces mailing labels from the survey tapes for businesses that sell products to schools. Ask for the center's *Directory of Computer Tapes.*

EQUAL EMPLOYMENT OPPORTUNITY COMMISSION (EEOC)

EEOC Survey Division
Office of Program
Research, Rm. 400
2401 E St., NW
Washington, DC 20507

The EEOC surveys employment in private industry every year, and its reports are categorized by sex, race, ethnic group, and broad job categories. Results are published for MSAs and larger geographical units.

CONTACT
James S. Neal
202-634-7062

WHAT YOU CAN GET FROM THE EEOC

Job Patterns for Minorities and Women

The following reports were available in early 1988:
Job Patterns for Minorities and Women...
1. ...in Private Industry, 1985
2. ...in Referral Unions, 1983
3. ...in State and Local Government, 1985
4. ...Elementary and Secondary School Staffing (using most current data)
5. ...in Colleges and Universities (using most current data)
 Single copies of the reports are available free of charge from the EEOC Survey Division.

HEALTH STATISTICS, National Center for

Scientific and Technical Information Branch
U.S. Dept. of Health and Human Services
3700 East-West Hwy.,
Room 157
Hyattsville, MD 20782

The National Center for Health Statistics was founded in 1960 to collect and disseminate data on health in the United States. Some of the center's statistics come from local registrations of births and deaths, marriages and divorces, but most come out of an extensive program of national surveys, usually conducted for the center by the Census Bureau or private survey firms.

CONTACT
Sandra Smith
301-436-8500
(See page 109 for Subject Specialists.)

FOR MORE INFORMATION
Catalogs listing the center's publications, reports and computer tapes are available for free from its Scientific and Technical Information Branch at the above address.

WHAT YOU CAN GET FROM THE NATIONAL CENTER FOR HEALTH STATISTICS

Annual Volumes, Vital Statistics of the United States

These reports contain final figures tabulated by natality, mortality, marriage and divorce for states, counties, metropolitan areas, and cities with populations of 10,000 or more. The data, which are published four years after they are collected, can be ordered from the Superintendent of Documents, Government Printing Office, Washington, DC 20402.

Monthly Vital Statistics Report

This report, with its annual summary, provides monthly and cumulative data, with brief analyses, on births, deaths, marriages, divorces, and infant deaths for states and the U.S. The final statistics are released about a year later in *Advance Reports*, available from the center at no charge.

Vital Statistics Surveys

Since the information contained on a birth, death, or marriage certificate is necessarily limited, the center supplements it by taking four broad surveys, the results of which are published in Vital and Health Statistics, available from the Superintendent of Documents.

1986 National Mortality Followback Survey

Covers risk factors associated with premature death, health services received and their cost during the last year of life, and lifestyles; e.g., diet, exercise, etc. Data from this survey will be available in late 1988 and you can get more information by calling the center at 301-436-7107.

National Mortality Survey (Series 20)

Mortality surveys, conducted annually from 1961 through 1968 and again in 1986, collected data on such topics as the smoking habits of people who had died between the ages of 35 and 84. Call the center at 301-436-8954 for more information.

National Natality Survey (Series 21)

The birth survey periodically studies pregnancy history, birth expectations, family composition, employment status, health insurance coverage, and related topics. Data from 1980 are currently available, and another survey will be taken in 1988.

National Survey of Family Growth (Series 23)

This survey, which was conducted in 1973, 1976, 1982, and 1988, gathers statistics about the dynamics of population change, family planning, and maternal and child health. Data on birth intentions and a range of demographic and economic variables are also reported. Data from the 1988 study will be available in the fall of 1989. For more information call 301-936-8731.

Health Interview Survey

This annual survey is the principal source of information on the health of Americans. It obtains statistics on health and demographic factors related to illness, injuries and disability, and the costs and uses of medical services. Information from this survey is published in Vital and Health Statistics, Series 10, available from the Superintendent of Documents.

Health and Nutrition Examination Survey

The data in this survey are collected through physical examinations as well as through interviews. The center sends out a mobile examination unit made up of specially constructed truck-drawn rooms. This way the center ensures that all examinations are uniform in temperature and humidity control for exercise tests and in noise levels for hearing tests. Information on this survey is published in Vital and Health Statistics, Series 11, available from the Superintendent of Documents.

Hispanic Health and Nutritional Examination Survey

This one-time survey of a sample of 16,000 Hispanics was conducted in 1982-84, and information from it was released in separate reports in Vital and Health Statistics, Series 11. Because the information published is so diverse, it is organized by topic, such as "cholesterol levels" or "periodontal disease." Available from the Superintendent of Documents.

Hospital Discharge Survey

This survey collects information annually on hospital patients' demographic characteristics, how long they stayed in the hospital, and the purpose of their visit. The data are published in Vital and Health Statistics, Series 13, available from the Superintendent of Documents.

National Ambulatory Medical Care Survey

A complement to the Hospital Discharge Survey, this survey is a continuous sample of patients' visits to doctors' offices. Doctors fill out forms for a sample of their patients, including their age, race, sex, principal problem, diagnosis, and treatment prescribed. Data from this survey, which is conducted every three years beginning in 1985, and was done annually from 1974 through 1984, are published in Vital and Health Statistics, Series 13, available from the Superintendent of Documents.

Nursing Home Survey

This national, intermittently-conducted survey, collects data on nursing home residents, staff, and facilities. The information is used for evaluating present legislation, such as Medicare and Medicaid, and for planning new legislation. The last survey was conducted in 1985-86 and data from it were released in 1987 in Series 13, Vital and Health Statistics, available from the Superintendent of Documents.

Computer Tapes Available

Computer tapes containing detailed data are available, and the center will also answer requests for unpublished data if it has already made the tabulations or, for a fee, it will make special tabulations. For further information call the Scientific and Technical Information Branch at 301-436-8500. To order tapes, contact the National Technical Information Service, 5285 Port Royal Road, Springfield, VA 22161; 703-487-4650. Most tapes are available at an average cost of $160.

HOUSING AND URBAN DEVELOPMENT, Department of

451 Seventh Street, NW
Washington, DC 20410

CONTACT
John Murphy
202-755-6374
(See page 109 for
Subject Specialists.)

An enormous amount of valuable data is provided by HUD's American Housing Survey, which updates changes in the housing inventory and the demographic characteristics of occupants. Conducted nationally every other year, separate samples of 11 of 44 selected MSAs are taken every year. Unlike the Census Bureau's Current Population Survey, the American Housing Survey returns to the same housing units, a practice that makes it possible to check for changes in a house.

WHAT YOU CAN GET FROM HUD

***American Housing
Survey Reports***

Published reports from the American Housing Survey National Sample (Series H-150) cover six basic subjects, each of which provides data for the U.S. and regions:

***A. General Housing
Characteristics***

This report provides data on tenure, vacancy rates, number of rooms, household race and composition, characteristics of newly constructed units, etc.

***B. Indicators of
Housing and
Neighborhood Quality***

Organized by financial characteristics, this report covers structural characteristics of dwelling units, such as water damage to roofs and basements, cracked and peeling paint or plaster, and holes in floors, ceilings, or walls.

***C. Financial
Characteristics of the
Housing Inventory***

Cross-tabulations of housing and demographic characteristics by income of families and individuals.

***D. Housing
Characteristics of
Recent Movers***

Reports data for households that moved into a unit within the previous 12 months. Reasons for moving and characteristics of the previous and current unit are presented.

**Other Housing
Survey Reports**

Two other reports which are available from the American housing survey are **Rural and Urban Housing Characteristics** and **Energy-Related Housing Characteristics**.

Other Reports

Other reports include the Summary of Housing Characteristics for Selected Metropolitan Areas (Series H-170), a supplementary report that shows selected occupancy, vacancy, utilization, structural, and financial characteristics. Printed reports from the 1985 survey will be available in the fall of 1988; order from the Superintendent of Documents, Government Printing Office, Washington, DC 20402.

Computer Tapes

Computer tapes from the 1985 American Housing Survey were available in the spring of 1988 and can be ordered from the Customer Services Branch, Data User Services Division, U.S. Bureau of the Census, Washington, DC 20233; 301-763-4100.

Computer tapes with individual response records are available from both the MSA and national samples. However, because of confidentiality guidelines, the tapes are available only for areas with large samples. Contact the Data User Services Division for more information.

Other Data Available

Before ordering tapes, you may also want to check with the Census Bureau for unpublished data, which are available either in paper photocopies or on microfiche. An index of what you can get is available free of charge from the Housing Division, U.S. Department of Commerce, Washington, DC 20233.

IMMIGRATION AND NATURALIZATION SERVICE

Statistical Analysis
Branch, Room 235
425 Eye Street, NW
Washington, DC 20536

Contact
Michael Hoefer
202-376-3066
(See page 109 for
Subject Specialists.)

Part of the Department of Justice, the Immigration &
Naturalization Service is the source of data about population change due to international migration. It gathers a
wide array of data for immigrants, nonimmigrants, refugees, people becoming naturalized citizens, and children
claiming citizenship through the naturalization of their
parents.

WHAT YOU CAN GET FROM THE
IMMIGRATION & NATURALIZATION SERVICE

*Nonimmigrant
Statistics*

This quarterly bulletin compares nonimmigrant and arriv-
ing visitor statistics with data from the same quarter of the
previous fiscal year. Includes port of entry statistics by
classification and port of departure. Order through the Immigration & Naturalization Service.

*The Statistical
Yearbook*

An annual yearbook which provides data about population
change due to international migration. Demographic data
include age, country of birth, occupation, country of last
permanent residence, marital status, sex, nationality, and
zip code of intended residence. The data also include
when, where, and under what status the individual entered
the country. Order from the National Technical Information Service, 5285 Port Royal Road, Springfield, VA
22161; 703-487-4650.

Tapes Available

The branch also puts together public-use tapes, which go
back ten years, making it easy to analyze trends. Available
from the National Technical Information Service.

INTERNAL REVENUE SERVICE

Statistics of Income Division, TR:S
1111 Constitution Avenue, NW
Washington, DC 20224

CONTACT
Fritz Scheuren
202-376-0216

The IRS Statistics of Income Division's annual report of individual income is a good source of demographic data between censuses. Income by income source, tax deductions, and tax exemptions are all reported by the marital status of the taxpayer. Researchers can usually infer household composition from the filing status of the taxpayer and the number of exemptions. Exemptions can also be used in making population inferences for years between censuses.

WHAT YOU CAN GET FROM THE IRS

Statistics of Income (SOI) Bulletin

This quarterly report is where the division reports its first statistics based on individual income tax returns for the year just past, and it is most useful for discerning trends, rather than levels of change in individual income. The *Bulletin* also provides estimates on the personal wealth of the nation's top wealthholders, tabulated by age, sex, and marital status. The *SOI Bulletin* is available for $16 from the Superintendent of Documents, Government Printing Office, Washington, DC 20402.

Individual Tax Model File

The microdata available in these public-use computer tapes often provide more detailed information than the printed publications, but some of the data are edited to protect the identity of individual taxpayers. Researchers can buy the Tax Model File from the IRS, which also sells two sets of files containing county-level migration data.

Other Services Available

For $32 you can buy a special package that includes a copy of the Statistics of Income Division's annual report, *Statistics of Income—Individual Income Tax Returns*, for a given year, and preliminary data for the two following income years. Order directly from the Statistics of Income Division of the IRS.

JUSTICE STATISTICS, Bureau of

633 Indiana Ave., NW
Washington, DC 20531
202-724-7759

Part of the Department of Justice, the Bureau of Justice Statistics provides data on both the victims of crime and its perpetrators.

CONTACT
Sue Lindgren
202-724-7759
(See page 109 for
Subject Specialists.)

FOR MORE INFORMATION
• Data Center Clearinghouse for Drugs & Crime Statistics; call 800-666-3332 for information and research service.
• Justice Statistics Clearinghouse; call 800-732-3277 for information and research service.
• *Telephone Contacts* lists a wide range of criminal justice topics and the names and telephone numbers of subject specialists. Available for free from the Superintendent of Documents, Government Printing Office, Washington, DC 20402.
• *How to Gain Access to BJS Data* describes the Bureau's programs and how to obtain data and services from it. Also available for free from the Superintendent of Documents.

WHAT YOU CAN GET FROM THE BJS

Correctional Statistics   A survey which collects age, race, sex, income, marital status, education, criminal, and drug use history data every five years on state prisoners and jail inmates.

National Crime Survey   Every six months, the National Crime Survey asks a sample of 49,000 Americans aged 12 and older in urban, suburban, and rural areas about their experience during the previous six months with rape, robbery, assault, household burglary, personal and household larceny, and motor vehicle theft.

   The survey provides data about the victim's demographics, where and when the crime occurred, the extent of injury and economic loss, the relationship between the victim and the person committing the crime, and whether or not the crime was reported and why. The survey also asks whether the offender was on drugs and asks victims to describe their experience with the criminal justice system.

Report to the Nation on Crime and Justice, Second Edition

This excellent publication is a non-technical report on crime and justice, and was regarded as a landmark document when first published.

Sourcebook of Criminal Justice Statistics

This annual book incorporates criminal justice data from virtually every source of national data, including public opinion surveys, the FBI, and the court system.

How to Order Reports

There are many other BJS reports available, and they're all free from the Justice Statistics Clearinghouse, Box 6000, Rockville, MD 20850. Outside of Maryland and Washington, DC, call toll-free 800-732-3277; Maryland and Washington, DC, call 301-251-5500.

Tapes also available

The Bureau of Justice Statistics places public-use tapes in the Criminal Justice Archive and Data Network of the Inter-University Consortium for Political and Social Research at the University of Michigan. Data tapes from the annual surveys are archived here too.

To order machine-readable data files, call the archive staff at 313-763-5010, or write CJAIN, P.O. Box 1248, Ann Arbor, MI 48106. This organization also puts out a free quarterly newsletter, the ICPSR Bulletin.

LABOR STATISTICS, Bureau of

441 G Street, NW
Washington, DC 20212

Most of the statistics that people need to assess what is going on in the economy—trends in prices, earnings, employment, unemployment, consumer spending, wages, and productivity—come from the Bureau of Labor Statistics.

CONTACT
Veola Kittrell
202-523-1221
(See page 110 for
Subject Specialists.)

FOR MORE INFORMATION

The following reports are free and can be obtained from the Office of Inquiries and Correspondence, U.S. Bureau of Labor Statistics, 441 G St., NW, Rm. 2831A, Washington, DC 20212; 202-523-1221 or 1222:

• *Major Programs of the Bureau of Labor Statistics,* which describes each of the agency's activities in detail and lists relevant publications.

• *BLS Update*, a quarterly publication which lists all new publications and tells how to get them.

• *Telephone Contacts for Data Users*, which lists the names and telephone numbers of all subject-matter specialists.

WHAT YOU CAN GET FROM THE BLS

*Consumer
Expenditure Survey*

This is the most detailed source of data on consumer spending. It consists of interviews and diaries from some 10,000 households which keep detailed records of their purchases for two-week periods throughout the year. Tables and tapes of the survey data are available on an annual basis, and people who are interested in getting data should contact the BLS to be put on the mailing list. The latest data available are from the 1986 survey.

*Current Population
Survey (CPS)*

Conducted every month by the Census Bureau, this survey is the bureau's major source of employment and demographic data. The CPS also gathers quarterly information on people's weekly earnings by demographic group and occupation. There are separate labor force reports for blacks and Hispanics, as well as for women. (For more details about the Current Population Survey, see page 68.) Available from the Superintendent of Documents, Government Printing Office, Washington, DC 20402.

Labor Force Projections	Every other year, the BLS projects the size and characteristics of the labor force as well as the demand for people in particular occupations and industries. These projections are based in part on the bureau's industry/occupation matrix, which is updated annually and is available on computer tape from the BLS.
Occupational Employment Statistics Survey	This annual survey covers each major industry division on a three-year cycle and the data are published in bulletins entitled "Occupational Employment in (Industry Division)." Available from the Superintendent of Documents.

THE BLS PUBLISHES SIX PERIODICALS

Described below, they're all available from the Superintendent of Documents, Government Printing Office, Washington, DC 20402.

The Monthly Labor Review	This venerable economics and social sciences publication features articles on employment, wages, prices, and productivity; $16 a year.
Employment and Earnings	Gives current employment and earnings statistics for the U.S., individual states, and over 200 areas. Included are household and establishment data, seasonally and not seasonally adjusted. Available for $22 a year, which includes an annual supplement.
Current Wage Developments	Reports on wage and benefit changes from collective bargaining agreements. Includes data on strikes or lockouts, major agreements expiring, and compensation changes; $12 a year.
CPI Detailed Report	Provides the monthly consumer price indexes and rates of change. It also includes data on commodity and service groups for 27 cities; $16 a year.

Occupational Outlook Quarterly	Helps students and guidance counselors learn about new occupations, training opportunities, salary trends, and career counseling programs. Written in nontechnical language and illustrated in color; $5 for four issues.
Producer Price Indexes	Includes price movement of industrial commodities and farm products each month. The $21 price includes an annual supplement.
Other useful BLS reports	"Employment in Perspective: Women in the Labor Force," "Employment in Perspective: Minority Workers," and the quarterly "Usual Weekly Earnings of Wages and Salary Workers." Order them from the Superintendent of Documents.
Tapes Available	*BLS Data Files on Tape* is available from the Bureau of Labor Statistics, Division of Special Publications, Washington, DC 20212; 202-523-1090. Requests for these tapes, which are available for the cost of duplication, should be addressed to the Bureau of Labor Statistics, Division of Financial Planning and Management, Washington, DC 20212.
News Releases Online	The BLS makes its news releases available online through a commercial contractor. There is no charge for the data; users pay only for actual computer time, which is about $7.50 an hour for local access and $20 an hour for access anywhere in the country. For more information write to the BLS Electronic News Release Service, 441 G St. NW, Rm. 2029, Washington, DC 20212.

NATIONAL TECHNICAL INFORMATION SERVICE

5285 Port Royal Road
Springfield, VA 22161

The National Technical Information Service sells information the government produces that can help U.S. businesses. Perhaps for this reason, NTIS is run like a business: It gets no money from Congress and must support itself from the sale of its products.

Customers can charge orders to their VISA, MasterCard, or American Express accounts, and for an extra fee you can get publications within 24 hours.

CONTACT
Stuart Weisman
703-487-4807
(See page 110 for Subject
Specialists.)

FOR MORE INFORMATION
NTIS General Catalog, available for free from NTIS Promotions Division, 5285 Port Royal Road, Springfield, VA 22161; 703-487-4812

WHAT YOU CAN GET FROM THE NTIS

Published Searches

Once NTIS has performed a custom search, it adds the search to its Published Search stock and lists it in its *Published Searches Catalog*. If a published search does not meet your needs, you can return it for credit against a custom search.

**How to Access the
NTIS Database**

The NTIS bibliographic database can be accessed through any of the following on-line services:
• Lockheed (DIALOG), 800-334-2564
• Systems Development Corporation (ORBIT) 800-421-7229
• STN International, 800-848-6533; 800-848-6538 in Ohio
• Bibliographic Retrieval Services, 800-833-4707
• Data Star, 800-221-7754

The NTIS database is also available on CD-ROM through the following vendors:
DIALOG, 800-334-2564
OCLC, 800-848-5878, 800-848-8286 in Ohio
Silver Platter, 800-343-0064

**NTIS Abstract
Newsletter**

The NTIS database is updated every two weeks, and people can keep up by subscribing to the weekly *NTIS Abstract Newsletter* in their area of interest, such as "Business and Economics," "Behavior and Society," and "Problem Solving Information for State and Local Governments." Whatever method you choose for finding out what material NTIS has, you can order reports in printed or micro form from the NTIS.

**Computer Tapes
Available**

The NTIS also sells computerized data files and software produced by federal agencies. For a listing by title, price, and order number, contact the Data Base Services Division at 703-487-4807.

SOCIAL SECURITY ADMINISTRATION

Office of Research & Statistics
U.S. Department of Health & Human Services
4301 Conn.Ave, N.W.
Washington, DC 20008

The best source of data on America's growing elderly population is the Social Security Administration, which puts out regular reports on the Old Age, Survivors, and Disability Insurance Program (Social Security), as well as the Supplemental Security Income (SSI), and Aid to Families with Dependent Children (AFDC) Programs.

CONTACT
Leila Finley
202-673-5620
(The SSA moved to a new building shortly after our publication deadline, so Ms. Finley's number may have changed; see page 110 for Subject Specialists.)

FOR MORE INFORMATION
The *SSA Research and Statistics Publications Catalog* and single copies of all documents in the catalog are available from the Office of Research and Statistics Publication staff.

WHAT YOU CAN GET FROM THE SOCIAL SECURITY ADMINISTRATION

Social Security Bulletin

This monthly publication has an annual supplement containing analytical articles and detailed statistical tables reflecting SSA programs. Topics covered include the poor population, sources of income for aged households, current living arrangements of persons 65 and older, and aged households receiving Social Security by race and the share of their income the benefits represent. The *Bulletin* provides data on workers by insured status, workers who are eligible for benefits, average monthly benefit amounts by type, and the estimated number of people in the Social Security population and the proportion fully insured. Quarterly data by state are available for a number of items. A subscription to the *Social Security Bulletin* can be ordered from the Superintendent of Documents, Government Printing Office, Washington, DC, for $23 a year. Supplements can be ordered separately for $15.

Social Security Beneficiaries by State and County, 1985

Contains the number of Social Security beneficiaries in each state and county, and the total dollar amount of benefits. Available from the Superintendent of Documents.

Social Security Beneficiaries by ZIP Code, 1985

Data on the amount of benefit payments are available for states and zip codes and give the number of Social Security beneficiaries by age, sex, and race. This report is published in ten volumes, and is available through the Social Security Administration.

Social Security Beneficiaries in Metropolitan Areas, 1983

The number of beneficiaries living in metropolitan areas is given by the type and amount of benefits received and by age, sex, and race. Available from the Social Security Administration.

The 1982 New Beneficiary Survey

This is a national survey of a sample of people who began receiving Social Security benefits between mid-1980 and mid-1981. The interview gathered basic demographic information, employment history, what conditions prevailed during the transition to retirement, and what conditions influenced the retirement decision. Interviewers also asked them to recount their childrearing history in order to estimate the impact of proposals to provide child care credits in the Social Security program. The results are available in reports and on a public-use computer tape. Orders should be sent to Joel Packman, Room 2-B-2, Operations Building, Social Security Administration, Baltimore, MD 21235.

Continuous Disability History Sample (CDHS)

This yearly restricted-use file contains data on about 20 percent of the people who filed for Social Security disability benefits, starting with 1975. The basic data cover personal characteristics, agency decision, payment history, and annual earnings.

VETERANS ADMINISTRATION

Office of Information
Management and
Statistics
Statistical Policy and
Research Service (71)
810 Vermont Ave., NW
Washington, DC 20420

The Office of Information Management and Statistics in the Veterans Administration produces and maintains a wealth of statistical data on the veteran population, including demographic, socioeconomic, and medical care information. The information is available in many reports, which are free and can be ordered by writing to the Veterans Administration.

CONTACT
Stephen Dienstfrey
202-233-3012
(See page 111 for
Subject Specialists.)

FOR MORE INFORMATION

Office of Information Management and Statistics Publications describes the many reports that are available from the VA. All publications from the Office of Information Management are available at the above address.

WHAT YOU CAN GET FROM THE VETERANS ADMINISTRATION

Below is a sample of reports available from the VA—they're all free and can be ordered by writing to the Office of Information Management and Statistics at the above address.

Data on Female Veterans
Contains statistical information on women veterans: population, health care, compensation and pension, and education. It's an annual report.

Veteran Population
A semiannual report containing estimates of the number of living veterans by period of military service, state of residence, VA regional office of jurisdiction, and age.

Current Health Status and the Future Demand for Health Care Programs and Social Support Services
A report based on the 1983 Survey of Aging Veterans, which was conducted by Louis Harris Associates for the VA. The report is especially valuable for healthcare planners and professionals.

Educational Attainment and Personal Income of Male Veterans and Nonveterans, March 1985
A report which contrasts the educational and income achievements of veterans and nonveterans over the decade. It further demonstrates how education is related to income for veterans and nonveterans and examines the extent to which income differences are attributed to differences in education as well as in age.

Administrator of Veterans Affairs Annual Report
Key subject areas on veterans are discussed in this report, and data are included on population, health care, compensation and pension, education benefits, cemeteries and memorials, and veterans assistance.

State and County Veteran Population
This report, published every two to three years, presents county-level estimates and forecasts.

Patient Treatment File
The PTF contains information on all episodes of patients discharged from VA medical centers, nursing homes, or domiciliaries during a given fiscal year. The file includes detailed data on patient characteristics as well as clinical data.

Annual Patient Census
The Office of Information Management and Statistics collects and disseminates information on the veteran population in this yearly sample of 20 percent of VA hospital inpatients and residents of domiciliaries, and a complete count of all patients in VA nursing homes. The data collected pertain to the numbers of patients and their characteristics as of one particular day in the year. Standard data items collected include date of birth, compensation and pension status, disability rating, period of service, date of admission, sex, marital status, race/ethnicity, and principal diagnosis.

SUBJECT CONTACTS at Federal Agencies

U.S. BUREAU OF THE CENSUS
U.S. Department of Commerce
Washington, DC 20233

Data User Services Division	Customer Services Staff	301-763-4100
Office of Congressional Affairs	Frederick A. Ruth, Chief	763-5360
Public Information Office	Staff	763-4040
1990 Census Promotional Office	Staff	763-1921

Demographic Programs

Center for Demographic Studies	James R. Wetzel, Chief	301-763-7720
Center for International Research	Barbara Boyle Torrey, Chief	763-2870
Decennial Operations Division	Arnold A. Jackson, Chief	763-5613
Decennial Planning Division	Susan M. Miskura, Chief	763-7670
Demographic Surveys Division	Thomas C. Walsh, Chief	763-2776
Geography Division	Robert W. Marx, Chief	763-5636
Housing Division	Acting Chief	763-2863
International Statistical Programs Center	Robert O. Bartram, Chief	763-2832
Population Division	Paula Schneider, Chief	763-7646
Statistical Methods Division	Preston Jay Waite, Chief	763-2672
Statistical Support Division	Acting Chief	763-7802

Population, Housing & Geographic Subjects

Age and Sex (U.S., States)	Staff	301-763 -5072
Age Search	Census History Staff	763-7936
Aging Population	Cynthia Taeuber	763-7883
Apportionment	Robert Speaker	763-7955
Citizenship: Foreign Born/Stock, Country of Birth	Nancy Sweet	763-7571
Commuting: Means of Transportation, Place of Work	Phil Salopek	763-3850
Consumer Expenditure Survey	Gail Hoff	763-2063
Crime Surveys: Victimization, General Information	Larry McGinn	763-1735
Current Population Survey	Kathleen Creighton	763-2773
Decennial Census:		
Content & Tabulations–Program Design	Patricia Berman	763-2358
Count Questions–1990 Census	Edgar Elam	763-2685
Content (General)	Al Paez/P. Lichtman-Panzer	763-5987/5270
Tabulations and Publications (General)	Cheryl Landman/Gloria Porter	763-3938/4908
Special Tabulations:		
Housing Data	Bill Downs	763-2873
Population Data	Phil Fulton	763-7962
1980 Counts for Current Boundaries	Joel Miller	763-1996

Disability	Jack McNeil	301-763-7946
Education, School Enrollment		
and Social Stratification	Paul Siegel	763-1154
Employment, Unemployment,		
Labor Force	Thomas Palumbo/Gordon Lester	763-2825
Farm Population:		
Census, Current Surveys	Diana DeAre	763-3850
Fertility/Births, Number of	Martin O'Connell/Amara Bachu	763-5303
Geographic Concepts and Products:		
Area Measurement	Robert Durland	763-1779
Boundaries of Legal Areas:		
Annexations, Boundary Changes	Nancy Goodman	763-3827
State Boundary Certification	Louise Stewart	763-3827
Census Geographic Concepts	Staff	763-5720
Census Tracts:		
Address Allocations	Ernie Swapshur	763-5720
Boundaries, Codes, Delineation	Cathy Miller	763-3827
Centers for Population	Don Hirschfeld	763-5720
Congressional Districts:		
Address Allocations	Ernie Swapshur	763-5692
Boundaries, Component Areas	Kevin Shaw	763-4667
Foreign Geography	Robert Durland	763-1779
GBF /DIME System	Staff	763-4664
Maps:		
1970/1980 Census Map Information	Larry Taylor	763-5720
1980 Census Map Orders	Leila Baxter	812-288-3192
1990 Census Map Plans	Sheldon Piepenburg	301-763-1580
Cartographic Operations	Staff	763-3973
Computer Mapping	Fred Broome	763-3973
Metropolitan Areas (MSAs)	Richard Forstall	763-5158
Outlying Areas	Staff	763-2903
Statistical Areas	Staff	763-3827
TIGER System Products	Sheldon Piepenburg	763-1580
Urban/Rural Residence	Staff	763-7955
Voting Districts	Virgeline Davis	763-3827
ZIP Codes	Rose Quarato	763-4667
Health Surveys	Robert Mangold	763-5508
Households Estimates for		
States and Counties	Campbell Gibson	763-1408
Household Wealth	Enrique Lamas	763-7946
Households and Families: Census,		
Current Surveys, Projections	Staff	763-7950
Housing:		
American Housing Survey	Edward Montfort	763-2880
Components of Inventory Change Survey	Jane Maynard	763-2880
Information, Decennial Census	Bill Downs	763-2873
Market Absorption/Residential Finance	Anne Smoler/Peter Fronczek	763-2866
New York City Housing &Vacancy Survey	Peter Fronczek	763-2866

Immigration (Legal/Undocumented), Emigration	Karen Woodrow	301-763-5590
Income Statistics	Staff	763-5060
Income Surveys	Chester Bowie	763-2764
Institutional Population	Denise Smith	763-7883
International Statistics:		
Africa, Caribbean, Latin America	Peter Way	763-4086
Asia, Oceania, Europe & North America	Arjun Adlakha	763-4221
China, People's Republic of	Judith Banister	763-4012
International Data Base	Peter Johnson	763-4811
Soviet Union	Barry Kostinksy	763-4022
Women in Development	Ellen Jamison	763-4221
Journey to Work	Phil Salopek	763-3850
Language, Current: Mother Tongue	Paul Siegel	763-1154
Longitudinal Surveys	Ronald Dopkowski	763-2767
Marital Status, Living Arrangements	Arlene Saluter	763-7950
Migration and Geographic Mobility:		
Current Statistics	Kristin Hansen/Celia Boertlein	763-3850
Occupation and Industry Statistics	John Priebe/Paula Vines	763-5144
(See also Economic Programs)		
Place of Birth	Kristin Hansen/Celia Boertlein	763-3850
Population:		
General Information, Published Data from Censuses, Surveys, Estimates, and Projections	Staff	763-5002 or 763-5020(TTY)
Population Estimates Methodology:		
Counties (total), MSAs, Places, Congressional Districts	Staff	763-7722/7964
Estimates Research:		
Race Estimates	David Word	763-7964
Experimental County Estimates by Age and Sex	Sam Davis	763-5072
United States, States by Age	Staff	763-5072
Population Projections Methodology	Edward Hanlon	763-1902
Poverty Statistics		
(Decennial Census & Current Surveys)	Staff	763-5790/7946
Prisoner Surveys:		
National Prisoner Statistics	Larry McGinn	763-1735
Race and Ethnic Statistics:		
Ethnic Populations	Nancy Sweet	763-7571
Race	Staff	763-2607/7572
Spanish Population	Carmen DeNavas/Arthur Cresce	763-5219
Reapportionment/Redistricting	Marshall Turner/Cathy Talbert	763-4686
Sampling Methods, Current Programs	Gary Shapiro	763-2674
Sampling Methods, Decennial Census	Richard Griffin	763-4154
Social Stratification	Paul Siegel	763-1154
Special Population Censuses	George Hum	763-7854

Special Surveys	Ronald Dopkowski	301-763-2767
SMSAs (Now MSAs)	Richard Forstall	763-5158
Survey of Income & Program Participation	Daniel Kaspryzk	763-5784
Travel Surveys	John Cannon	763-5468
Undercount:		
Demographic Analysis	Gregg Robinson	763-5590
Post-Enumeration Surveys	Howard Hogan	763-1794
Veterans Status	Thomas Palumbo/Gordon Lester	763-2825
Voting and Registration/Voting Rights	Jerry Jennings/Paul Siegel	763-4547/1154
Women	Cynthia Taeuber	763-7883

Economic Programs

Agriculture Division	Charles Pautler, Chief	301-763-5230
Business Division	Howard Hamilton, Chief	763-7564
Center for Economic Studies	Robert McGuckin, III, Chief	763-2337
Construction Statistics Division	Leonora M. Gross, Chief	763-7163
Economic Census Staff	Thomas Mesenbourg, Chief	763-7356
Economic Programming Division	Barry M. Cohen, Chief	763-2912
Economic Surveys Division	W. Joel Richardson, Chief	763-7735
Foreign Trade Division	Don L. Adams, Chief	763-5342
Governments Division	John R. Coleman, Chief	763-7366
Industry Division	Gaylord E. Worden, Chief	763-5850

Economic Subjects

Agriculture:

Crop Statistics	Donald Jahnke	301-763-1939
Data Requirements and Outreach	Douglas Miller	763-4164
Farm Economics	James A. Liefer	763-5819
General Information	Brenda Prout	763-1113
Irrigation and Horticulture Statistics	John Blackledge	763-4682
Livestock Statistics	Thomas Monroe	763-1081
Puerto Rico, Virgin Islands, Guam, No. Marianas	Kent Hoover	763-5656

Business Statistics:

Business Owner's Characteristics	Peggy Allen	763-5779
Minority and Women-Owned Businesses	Donna McCutcheon	763-5517
Retail Trade:		
Advance Monthly Sales, Annual Sales, Mo. Inventories	Ronald Piencykoski	763-5294
Census	Mark Wallace	763-7038
Monthly Retail Trade Report	Irving True	763-7128
Service Industries:		
Census	Sidney Marcus	763-7039
Current Selected Services Reports	Thomas Zabelsky	763-5528
Wholesale Trade:		
Census	John Trimble	763-5281
Current Wholesale and Inventories	Shirley Roberts	763-3916

Construction Statistics:

Census/Industries Surveys	Staff	301-763-7163
Special Trades, Contractors	Andrew Visnansky	763-7546
Construction Authorized by		
Building Permits (C40 Series)	Linda Hoyle	763-7244
Current Programs	William Mittendorf	763-7165
New Residential Construction:		
Characteristics, Price Index,		
Sales (C25/27 Series)	Steve Berman	763-7842
Housing Starts (C20 Series)		
Completions (C22 Series)	David Fondelier/Stanley Rolark	763-5731
In Selected MSAs (C21 Series)	Dale Jacobson	763-7842
Survey of Expenditures for Residential		
Upkeep & Improvements (C50 Series)	George Roff	763-5705
Vacancy Data	Paul P. Harple, Jr.	763-2880
Value of New Construction Put in		
Place (C30 Series)	Allan Meyer	763-5717
County Business Patterns	Faran E. Stoetzel	763-5430
Employment/Unemployment Statistics	Thomas Palumbo/Gordon Lester	763-2825
Enterprise Statistics	Johnny Monaco	763-1758
Foreign Owned U.S. Firms	Jerry McDonald	763-5182
Foreign Trade Data Services	Staff/Minnie M. Davis	763-5140/7754
Geographic Areas of the		
Economic Censuses	Staff	763-4667

Governments:

Criminal Justice Statistics	Diana Cull	763-7789
Eastern States Government Sector	Genevieve Speight	763-7783
Employment	Alan Stevens	763-5086
Federal Expenditure Data	David Kellerman	763-5276
Finance	Henry Wulf	763-7664
Government Organization	Diana Cull	763-7789
Single Audit	William Fanning	763-4403
Taxation	Gerard Keffer	763-2858
Western States Government Sector	Ulvey Harris	763-5344

Income/Poverty

(See *Demographic Programs, Income Statistics and Income Surveys*)

Industry and Commodity Classification	C. Harvey Monk, Jr.	763-1935

Manufacturing:

Industry Data:	John P. Govoni	763-7666
Durables	Kenneth Hansen	763-7304
Nondurables	Michael Zampogna	763-2510
Products Data:	Robert Tinari	763-1924
Durables (Current Industrial Reports)	Malcolm Bernhardt	763-2518
Durables (Census/Annual Survey)	Kenneth Hansen	763-7304
Nondurables (Current Industrial Reports)	Staff	763-5911
Nondurables (Census/Annual Survey)	Michael Zampogna	763-2510

Special Topics:

Concentration, Origin of Exports	Bruce Goldhirsch	301-763-1503
Fuels/Electric Energy Consumed and Water Use	John McNamee	763-5938
Monthly Shipments, Inventories, Orders	Ruth Runyan	763-2502
Research and Development, Capacity, Production Index, Pollution Abatement	Elinor Champion	763-5616
Mineral Industries	John McNamee	763-5938

Puerto Rico, Virgin Islands, Guam:

Censuses of Retail Trade, Wholesale Trade, Selected Service Industries, Agriculture, Construction and Manufactures	Carl Bostrom/Kent Hoover	763-7240/5656
Quarterly Financial Report	Paul Zarrett	763-2718
Accounting and Related Issues	Ronald Lee	763-4270
Classification	Frank Hartman	763-4274

Transportation:

Commodity Transportation Survey, Truck Inventory and Use	Robert Crowther	763-4364

User Services, Statistical Standards & Methodology

Center for Survey Methods Research	Elizabeth A. Martin, Chief	301-763-3838
Data User Services Division	Gerard C. Iannelli, Chief	763-5820
Field Division	Stanley D. Matchett, Chief	763-5000
Statistical Research Division	Kirk M. Wolter, Chief	763-3807
Age Search–Access to Personal Census Records	Census History Staff	763-7936
Catalog, Bureau of the Census	John McCall	763-1584
CENDATA	Staff	763-2074
Census Awareness Products & Programs (Regional Offices)	Staff	763-5830
Census Curriculum Support Project	Staff	763-1510
Census Procedures, History of	Frederick Bohme	763-7936
Clearinghouse of Census Data Services	John Kavaliunas	763-1580
Computer Tapes, CD-ROM, Diskettes, etc.	Customer Service	763-4100
Data User News (Monthly Newsletter)	Neil Tillman	763-1584
Data User Training	Dorothy Chin	763-1510
Exhibits, Conventions	Joanne Dickinson	763-2370
Guides and Directories	Gary Young	763-1584
Microfiche	Customer Services	763-4100
Monthly Product Announcement	Bernice L. Baker	763-1584
Population Information	Staff	763-5002/5020
Public-Use Microdata Samples	Carmen Campbell	763-2005
Publication Orders	Customer Service	763-4100
State Data Center Program	Larry Carbaugh	763-1580
Statistical Abstracts:	Glenn King	763-5299
County & City, State & Metropolitan Area Data Books	Wanda Cevis	763-1034
Statistical Research for Demographic Programs	Lawrence Ernst	763-7880

Statistical Research for Economic Programs	Nash J. Monsour	301-763-5702
Undercount Research	Howard Hogan	763-1794
User Software (CENSPAC, etc.)	Staff	763-4100

Regional Assistance

ATLANTA	James F. Holmes, Dir.	404-347-2271
	Census Awareness & Products	404-347-2274
BOSTON	Arthur G. Dukakis, Dir.	617-565-7100
	Census Awareness & Products	617-565-7078
CHARLOTTE	William F. Hill, Dir.	704-371-6142
	Census Awareness & Products	704-371-6144
CHICAGO	Stanley D. Moore, Dir.	312-353-6251
	Census Awareness & Products	312-353-0980
DALLAS	Acting Director	214-767-7488
	Census Awareness & Products	214-767-7105
DENVER	William F. Adams. Dir.	303-969-7750
	Census Awareness & Products	303-969-7750
DETROIT	Acting Director	313-354-4654
	Census Awareness & Products	313 354-4654
KANSAS CITY	Marvin Postma, Dir.	913-236-3728
	Census Awareness & Products	816-891-7562
LOS ANGELES	John Reeder, Dir.	213-209-6616
	Census Awareness & Products	213-209-6612
NEW YORK	Sheila Grimm, Dir.	212-264-3860
	Census Awareness & Products	212-264-4730
PHILADELPHIA	LaVerne Vines Collins, Dir.	215-597-4920
	Census Awareness & Products	215-597-8313
SEATTLE	Leo C. Schilling, Dir.	206-442-7828
	Census Awareness & Products	206-442-7080

AGRICULTURE, Department Of
1301 New York Avenue, NW
Washington, DC 20005

Economic Research Service	James Sayre	202-786-1512
Family Economics Research	Helene Gutman	301-436-8461
Group Childraising Costs	Nancy Schwenk	436-8461
Human Nutrition Information Service	Laura Sims	436-8474
Income Studies Group	Thomas Carlin	202-786-1527
Information Division	Ben Blankenship	786-1504
Population Group	Calvin Beale	786-1534
Savings & Investment/Household Production	Colien Hefferan	301-436-8461

ECONOMIC ANALYSIS, Bureau of

U.S. Department of Commerce
1401 K Street, NW
Washington, DC 20230

Public Information Office	Larry Moran	202-523-0777
Computer Tape Requests		
(for regional projections)	Elizabeth Rozycki	523-0936
Economic Projections, State &		
Migration Patterns	Bruce Levine	523-0938
Personal Income & Employment,		
State, MSA & County Data Requests		
Regional Economic Information System Staff		523-0966
Small Area Information	Kenneth Johnson	523-0971

EDUCATION STATISTICS, Center for

Education Information Branch
U.S. Dept. of Education
555 New Jersey Avenue, NW
Washington, DC 20208

Information

Fred Beamer, Norman Brandt, Vance Grant, Richard Whalen		800-424-1616
In metro Washington area		800-626-9854
Adult Education	Susan Hill	202-357-6584
Common Core of Data	George Wade	357-6611
Data Tapes/Computer Products	Imelda Smallwood	357-6528
	John Dusatko	357-6522
Elementary & Secondary Education	Paul Planchon	357-6614
Longitudinal Studies	Dennis Carroll	357-6765
International Education	Larry Suter	357-6729
Library Surveys	Milton Chorvinsky	357-6729
Post-Secondary Education	Samuel Peng	357-6354
Private Schools	Jeffrey Williams	357-6325
Projections	Debra Gerald	357-6581
School District Tabulation	Richard Cook	357-6611
Vocational Education	Marjorie Chandler	357-6397

EQUAL EMPLOYMENT OPPORTUNITY COMMISSION (EEOC)

EEOC Survey Division
Office of Program Research
2401 E St., NW, Rm. 400
Washington, DC 20507   James S. Neal   202-634-7062/7063/7064

HEALTH STATISTICS, National Center for
Scientific and Technical Information Branch
U.S. Department of Health and Human Services
3700 East-West Highway, Room 157
Hyattsville, MD 20782

Contacts can all be reached at 301-436-8500, 6145, or 6155

Ambulatory Medical Care Survey	Linda Washington
Health and Nutrition Examination Survey	Linda Washington, Paula Summerour
Health Interview Survey	Linda Washington, Paula Summerour
Hospital Discharge Survey	Thomas Kubeck, Sharon Ramirez, Kathy Santini
Nursing Home Survey	Thomas Kubeck, Sharon Ramirez, Kathy Santini
Vital Statistics	Thomas Kubeck

HOUSING AND URBAN DEVELOPMENT, Department of
451 Seventh Street, NW
Washington, DC 20410

American Housing Survey	Kathy Nelson	202-755-5060
Information Policies and Systems	John Murphy	755-6374

IMMIGRATION AND NATURALIZATION SERVICE
Statistical Analysis Branch
425 Eye Street, NW, Tariff Room 235
Washington, DC 20536

Deportations, Required Departures & Exclusions	John Bjerke	202-376-3015
Expatriations	Robert Warren	376-3008
Immigrants	Michael Hoefer	376-3066
Nonimmigrants	Mark Herrenbruck	376-3015
Refugees, Naturalization & Derivative Citizenship	Christine Davidson	376-3046

INTERNAL REVENUE SERVICE
Statistics of Income Division, TR:S
1111 Constitution Avenue, NW
Washington, DC 20224   Fritz Scheuren   202-376-0216

JUSTICE STATISTICS, Bureau of
633 Indiana Avenue, NW
Washington, DC 20531

Correctional Statistics	Larry Greenfield	202-724-7755
Judicial Statistics	Patrick Langan	724-7774

| Law Enforcement Statistics | Paul White | 202-724-7770 |
| National Crime Survey | Patsy Klaus | 724-7774 |

LABOR STATISTICS, Bureau of
441 G Street, NW
Washington, DC 20212

Inquiries & Correspondence	Veola Kittrell	202-523-1221
Recorded Message: Consumer Price		
Index (CPI), Producer Price Indexes (PPI), & Employment Situation		523-9658
Consumer Expenditure Survey		
Data & Tapes	Stephanie Shipp	272-5060
Consumer Expenditure Surveys	Eva Jacobs	272-5156
Consumer Price Index Detail		523-1239
Demographic Studies	Paul Flaim	523-1944
Economic Growth and Employment		
Projections	Howard Fullerton	272-5328
Family & Marital Characteristics of		
Labor Force	Howard Hayghe	523-1371
Industry Occupational Employment Matrix	Delores Turner	272-5283
Local Area Unemployment Statistics	Carol Utter	523-1002
Microdata Tapes & Analysis	Robert McIntire	523-1776
Occupational Employment Statistics Survey	Michael McElroy	523-1684
Occupational Outlook	Michael Pilot	272-5282
Occupational Projections—National	Neal Rosenthal	272-5382
Producer Price Index detail		523-1765
State & Local Area Demographic Data	Edna Biederman	523-1002

NATIONAL TECHNICAL INFORMATION SERVICE
5285 Port Royal Road
Springfield, VA 22161

Bibliographic Data Base Searches		703-487-4640
Data Base Services	Stuart Weisman	487-4807
Promotions Division (call for free publications)		487-4812
Published Searches	Marie Lawall	487-4929
Sales Desk		487-4650

SOCIAL SECURITY ADMINISTRATION
Office of Research & Statistics
U.S. Department of Health & Human Services
4301 Connecticut Ave, N.W.
Washington, DC 20008

(Some of the following specialists moved to a new building just after our publication deadline, so their phone numbers may have changed.)

24-Hour Ordering Service		202-673-5209
Continuous Work History Sample	Warren Buckler	301-594-0324
	Creston Smith	301-594-0361
Disability Studies	Malcolm Morrison	301-965-0091
Economic & Long-Range Studies	Ben Bridges	202-673-5644
Family Support Administration	Emmett Dye	202-245-2743
International Policy, Office of	Libby Singleton	202-673-5655
Program Analysis Division	Martynas Ycas	202-673-5694
Retirement & Survivor Studies	Wayne Finager	301-965-7864
Statistical Analysis, Division of	Jack Schmulowitz	301-965-0179
Statistical Operations & Services, Div. of	Warren Buckler	301-594-0324

VETERANS ADMINISTRATION

Office of Information Management and Statistics
Statistical Policy and Research Service (71)
810 Vermont Avenue, NW
Washington, DC 20420

Administrator of Veterans' Affairs		
Annual Report	Dino Bernes	202-233-2525
Patient Treatment File & Annual		
Patient Census	Susan Gee Krumhaus	233-3930
Population Estimates & Forecasts,		
Surveys of Veterans	Stephen Dienstfrey	233-3012
Veterans Receiving Compensation or		
Pension & Veterans Receiving		
Educational Benefits	Mike Wells	233-3930

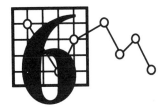

STATE AND LOCAL SOURCES

THESE ORGANIZATIONS USUALLY PROVIDE AT LEAST state-level information on population, economics, and vital statistics (births, deaths, marriages, and divorces). They also often have data for smaller areas, such as counties and cities.

Because they are frequently in a government office of a state or city, they may be the place to go if you want information that is based on intimate local knowledge of an area. Many state sources also have computer capabilities to do custom analysis of government data for you. Finally, the organizations listed under "State and Local Economic Information" have Bureau of Economic Analysis user groups.

Alabama

State Data Centers
Alabama State Data Center
for Business and Economic Research
University of Alabama
P.O. Box AK
Tuscaloosa, AL 35487
Annette Watters
205-348-6191
(The main branch of the state data
center also provides state estimates,
projections, and economic information.)

State Data Center
Alabama Department of Economic
and Community Affairs
3465 Norman Bridge Road
P.O. Box 2939
Montgomery, AL 36105-0939
Gilford C. Gilder
205-284-8778
(Also provides state estimates and pro-
jections.)

Alabama Public Library Service
6030 Monticello Drive
Montgomery, AL 36130
Blane K. Dessy
205-277-7330

State & Local Economic Information
Research & Statistics
State of Alabama
Dept. of Industrial Relations
649 Monroe Street
Montgomery, AL 36130
Douglas Dyer, Chief

Center for Business & Economic
Research
College of Business & Management
University of South Alabama
Mobile, AL 36688
Semoon Chang, Director
205-460-6156

Alabama Department of Economic and
Community Affairs
c/o State Capitol
Montgomery, AL 36130
Gil Gilder
205-284-8778

Vital Statistics
Bureau of Vital Statistics
State Department of Public Health
Montgomery, AL 36130

Local Demographic Information
The Birmingham News
P.O. Box 2553
Birmingham, AL 35202
Thomas M. Adams
205-325-2134

Alaska

State Data Centers
Alaska State Data Center
Alaska Department of Labor
P.O. Box 25504
Juneau, AK 99802-5504
Gregory Williams
907-465-4500
(The main branch of the state data
center also provides state estimates and
projections.)

Office of the Governor
Office of Management & Budget
Pouch AD
Juneau, AK 99811
Thomas Chester
907-465-3573

Department of Education
Alaska State Library
Pouch G
Juneau, AK 99811
Lou Coatney
907-465-2927

Dept. of Community & Reg. Affairs
Div. of Local Govt. Assistance
Pouch BH
Juneau, AK 99811
Paul Cunningham
907-465-4750

Alaska Department of Labor
Research & Analysis
P.O. Box 25501
Juneau, AK 99802-5501
Charles Caldwell, Chief
Greg Williams, State Demographer
(Also provides estimates, projections,
state and local economic information.)

State Projections
Institute for Social Economic &
Government Research
University of Alaska
707 A Street, Suite 206
Anchorage, AK 99501
Jack Kruse/Edward Gorsuch
907-278-4621

State & Local Economic Information
Division of Budget & Management
Office of the Governor
Pouch AM
Juneau, AK 99811-0164
Gregg K. Erickson
907-465-3568

Vital Statistics
Bureau of Vital Statistics
Department of Health & Social Services
P.O. Box H
Juneau, AK 99811-0675

Arizona

State Data Centers
Arizona Department of Economic
Security
Population Statistics Unit 1
300 W. Washington, 1st Floor

P.O. Box 6123, Site Code 045Z
Phoenix, AZ 85005
Linda Strock/Betty Jeffries
602-255-5984
(The main branch of the state data
center also provides state estimates and
projections.)

State Data Center/ASU
Bureau of Business and Economic
Research
College of Business Administration
Arizona State University
Tempe, AZ 85287
Timothy D. Hogan, Director
602-965-3961
(Also provides state and local economic
information.)

College of Business Administration
Northern Arizona University
Box 15066
Flagstaff, AZ 86011
Ronald Gunderson
602-523-7358
(Also provides state and local economic
information.)

Federal Documents Section
Department of Library, Archives &
Public Records
Capitol Bldg., Third Floor
1700 West Washington
Phoenix, AZ 85007
Janet Fisher
602-255-4121

University of Arizona
University Library
Government Documents
Tucson, AZ 85721
Cynthia Bower
602-621-6433

Research Administration
P.O. Box 6123-Site Code 733A
Phoenix, AZ 85005
Dan Anderson
602-255-3871
(Also provides state estimates, projections, and economic information.)

State & Local Economic Information
Division of Economic & Business
Research
University of Arizona
Tucson, AZ 85721
Nat De Gennaro
602-621-2155

Executive Research
Fourth Floor, Capitol Building
1700 West Washington
Phoenix, AZ 85007
Larry Landry
602-255-4331

Vital Statistics
Office of Planning & Health Status
Monitoring
Arizona Department of Health Services
1740 West Adams - Room 312
Phoenix, AZ 85007

Local Demographic Information
Phoenix Newspapers, Inc.
P.O. Box 1950
Phoenix, AZ 85001
Ellen Baar Jacobs
602-271-8870

Arkansas

State Data Centers
Research and Public Service
University of Arkansas at Little Rock
2801 South University
Little Rock, AR 72204
Sarah Breshears
501-371-1973

(The main branch of the state data
center also provides state estimates and
projections.)

Arkansas State Library
1 Capitol Mall
Little Rock, AR 72201
Mary Honeycatt
501-682-2864

State & Local Economic Information
Research & Public Service
University of Arkansas at Little Rock
33rd & University Avenue
Little Rock, AR 72204
Frank Troutman
501-371-1976 or 1977

Employment Security Division
Arkansas Department of Labor
State Capitol Mall
P.O. Box 2981
Little Rock, AR 72203
Herman Sanders
501-371-1541

Bureau of Business & Economic
Research
College of Business Administration
University of Arkansas
Fayetteville, AR 72701
Phillip Taylor
501-575-4151

Vital Statistics
Division of Vital Records
Arkansas Department of Health
4815 West Markham Street
Little Rock, AR 72205-3867

California

State Data Centers
Population Research Unit
State Department of Finance
1025 P Street

Sacramento, CA 95814
Linda Gage, Chief
916-322-4651
(The main branch of the state data
center also provides state estimates and
projections.)

Institute of Governmental Studies
University of California
Berkeley, CA 94720
Jack Leister Head Librarian
Eugene Lee, Director
415-642-1472
(Also provides state and local economic
information.)

State Data Program
University of California
Survey Research Center
2538 Channing Way
Berkeley, CA 94720
Ilona Einowski/Ann Gerken
415-642-6571

State & Local Economic Information
Center for Business & Economic
Research
California State University
Chico, CA 95926
Richard Davis, Director
916-895-5711

Business Forecasting Project
Graduate School of Management
University of California
Los Angeles, CA 90024
Larry J. Kimbell, Director
213-825-1623

State Department of Finance
1025 P Street, Room 325
Sacramento, CA 95814
Pauline Sweezey
916-322-2263

Vital Statistics
Health Data & Statistics Branch

Department of Health Services
714 P Street, Room 1494
Sacramento, CA 95814

Local Demographic Information
Sacramento Bee
P.O. Box 15779
Sacramento, CA 95852
Ronald M. Olsen
916-321-1407

The Press-Enterprise
P.O. Box 792
Riverside, CA 92502
Jeffery A. Mahan
714-0684-1200

The Sacramento Union
301 Capitol Mall
Sacramento, CA 95814
Susan S. Kossack
916-440-0303

Los Angeles Times
Times Mirror Square
Los Angeles, CA 90053
John Mount
213-237-5965

Orange County Register
625 N. Grand Avenue
P.O. Box 11626
Santa Ana, CA 92711
Robert Olinto
714-953-7963

Long Beach Press-Telegram
604 Pine Avenue
Long Beach, CA 90844
Carol Ragan
213-499-1435

Colorado

State Data Centers
Division of Local Government

Department of Local Affairs
1313 Sherman Street, Room 520
Denver, CO 80203
Reid T. Reynolds, State Demographer
Rebecca Picaso, Staff Assisstant
303-866-2156
(The main branch of the state data
center also provides state estimates,
projections, and economic information.)

Division of Business Research
Graduate School of Business and
Administration
University of Colorado
Campus Box 420
Boulder, CO 80309
C.R. Goeldner
303-492-8227
(Also provides state and local economic
information.)

Documents Department
The Libraries
Colorado State University
Fort Collins, CO 80523
Karen Jacob
303-491-1880

County Information Service
Agricultural and Resource Economics
Colorado State University
Fort Collins, CO 80523
Sue Anderson
303-491-5706

State & Local Economic Information
Labor Market Information Branch
Department of Labor and Employment
251 East 12th Avenue
Denver, CO 80203
Kenneth Anderson
303-620-4554

Vital Statistics
Health Statistics Section
Colorado Department of Health
4210 East 11th Avenue
Denver, CO 80220

Local Demographic Information
Rocky Mountain News
P.O. Box 719
Denver, CO 80201
Pam Michener
303-892-5485

The Denver Post
650 15th Street
Denver, CO 80202
Joan M. Robertson
303-820-1500

Connecticut

State Data Center
Comprehensive Planning Division
Office of Policy and Management
State of Connecticut
80 Washington Street
Hartford, CT 06106-4459
Theron A. Schnure
203-566-8285
(The main branch of the state data
center also provides state projections
and economic information.)

State Estimates
Division of Health Statistics
State Department of Health Services
150 Washington Street
Hartford, CT 06106
Lloyd Mueller
203-566-5451

State & Local Economic Information
Research & Information
Employment Security Division
Connecticut Labor Department
200 Folly Brook Boulevard
Wethersfield, CT 06109
Roger Skelly, Director
203-566-2120

Vital Statistics
Vital Records Section
Div. of Health Statistics
State Department of Health Services
150 Washington Street
Hartford, CT 06106

Local Demographic Information
The Day
P.O. Box 1231
New London, CT 06320
Fred Hebert
203-442-2200, ext. 290

The Hartford Courant
285 Broad Street
Hartford, CT 06115
John J. Burnett
203-241-6273

The Jackson Newspapers
40 Sargent Drive
New Haven, CT 06511
Susan E. Eckert
203-562-1121, ext. 417

Delaware

State Data Centers
Delaware Development Office
99 Kings Highway
P.O. Box 1401
Dover, DE 19903
Douglas Clendaniel/Judy Cherry
302-736-4271
(The main branch of the state data
center also provides state estimates,
projections, and economic information.)

Academic Computing Services
University of Delaware
Smith Hall
Newark, DE 19716
Bob Shaffer
302-451-1987

College of Urban Affairs Library
University of Delaware
Newark, DE 19716
Mary Helen Callahan
3020451-2394
(Also provides state estimates, projec-
tions, and vital statistics.)

Reference Department
University of Delaware Library
Newark, DE 19717-5267
Rebecca Knight
302-451-2965
(This Federal Depository Library also
provides state and local economic
information.)

State & Local Economic Information
Delaware Department of Labor
P.O. Box 9029
Newark, DE 19711
James K. McFadden
302-368-6962

Vital Statistics
Office of Vital Statistics
Division of Public Health
P.O. Box 637
Dover, DE 19903

District of Columbia

Data Centers
Data Services Division
D.C. Office of Planning
Presidential Building
Suite 314, 415 12th Street, NW
Washington, DC 20004
Albert Mindlin/Gangu Ahuja
202-727-6533
(Also provides estimates, projections,
and economic information.)

Metropolitan Washington Council of
Governments

1875 Eye Street, NW, Suite 200
Washington, DC 20006-5454
Paul Desjardin
202-223-6800, ext. 399
(Also provides economic information.)

Projections
Office of Economic Growth & Employment Projections
Bureau of Labor Statistics
Department of Labor
Washington, DC 20212
Howard N. Fullerton
202-272-5328

Population Projections Branch
Population Division
Bureau of the Census
Washington, DC 20233
301-763-1902

Projections Branch
Regional Economic Analysis Division
Bureau of Economic Analysis 14th & K
Streets, NW
Washington, DC 20230
Ken Johnson
202-523-0971

Economic Information
Economic & Tax Policy
Department of Finance & Revenue
Municipal Center, Room 4130
300 Indiana Avenue, NW
Washington, DC 20001
Mark I. Gripentrog
202-727-6027

Vital Statistics
Vital Records Branch
425 I Street, NW
Washington, DC 20001

Marriage Bureau
Superior Court of D.C.
500 Indiana Ave., NW, Rm. 4485
Washington, DC 20001

Clerk, Superior Court for the
District of Columbia
500 Indiana Avenue, NW
Washington, DC 20001

Florida

State Data Center
Executive Office of the Governor
Office of Planning & Budget
The Capitol
Tallahassee, FL 32301
Leslei Street-Hazlett
904-487-2814

State & Local Economic Information
Bureau of Economic & Business
Research
221 Matherly Hall
University of Florida
Gainesville, FL 32611
Stanley K. Smith, Program Director
904-392-0171
(Also provides state estimates and
projections.)

Executive Office of the Governor
O.P.B. Revenue & Economic Analysis
The Capitol
Tallahassee, FL 32399-0001
904-487-2814

Research & Statistics
Florida Department of Labor
Caldwell Building
Tallahassee, FL 32306
Pacharee Haspar, Chief
904-488-1048

Department of Economics
University of Miami
P.O. Box 248126
Coral Gables, FL 33124
Al Holtman, Chairman
305-284-5540

Bureau of Economic Analysis
Florida Department of Commerce
Room 407 Fletcher Building
Tallahassee, FL 32301
Gail Cruce
904-487-2971

Vital Statistics
Department of Health and
Rehabilitative Services
Office of Vital Statistics
P.O. Box 210
Jacksonville, FL 32231

Local Demographic Information
The Orlando Sentinel
P.O. Box 2833
Orlando, FL 32802
Jim Jackson
305-420-5790

Florida Publishing Co.
P.O. Box 1949F
Jacksonville, FL 32231
Wallace Parker
904-359-4524

St. Petersburg Times-Independent
P.O. Box 1121
St. Petersburg, FL 33731
Jane Peppard
813-893-8451

The Palm Beach Post
P.O. Box 24700
West Palm Beach, FL 33416-4700
Suzanne Willcox
305-837-4274

Miami Herald Publishing Co.
One Herald Plaza
Miami, FL 33132
Jack N. O'Hearn, Jr.
305-376-2791

Tampa Tribune
P.O. Box 191
Tampa, FL 33601
Theodore Stasney
813-272-7766

Georgia

State Data Centers
Governor's Office of Planning and
Budget
270 Washington Street, SW, Rm. 608
Atlanta, GA 30334
Thomas Wagner/Robin Kirkpatrick
404-656-0911
(The main branch of the state data
center also provides state estimates and
projections.)

Pullen Library-Reference Department
Georgia State University
100 Decatur St., SE
Atlanta, GA 30303
Gayle Christian, Reference/Documents
Librarian
404-651-2185

Main Library
University of Georgia
Athens, GA 30602
404-542-8949

Georgia Department of Community
Affairs
Government Information Division
1200 Equitable Building
100 Peachtree Street
Atlanta, GA 30303
Paul W. Lycett
404-656-5526

State Data Center Program
Albany State College
504 College Drive
Albany, GA 31705
Documents Librarian
912-439-4065

Data Services
University of Georgia Libraries
Athens, GA 30602
Hortense L. Bates
404-542-5242

State Data Center Program
Mercer University Law Library
Mercer University
Macon, GA 31207
Reynold Kosek
912-745-6811

Price Gilbert Memorial Library
Georgia Institute of Technology
Atlanta, GA 30332
Richard Leacy
404-894-4519

State & Local Economic Information
Georgia Dept. of Industry & Trade
P.O. Box 1776
Atlanta, GA 30301
Gloria A. Hardnett
404-656-3584

Labor Information Systems
Georgia Department of Labor
254 Washington Street, SW
Atlanta, GA 30334
Joyce A. Morris/Milton Martin
404-656-3177

Division of Research
University of Georgia
Athens, GA 30602
Albert Niemi, Jr.
404-542-4085

Economic Forecasting Center
Georgia State University
University Plaza
Atlanta, GA 30303
Donald Ratajczak, Director
404-651-3282

Vital Statistics
Department of Human Resources
Vital Records Unit
Room 217-H
47 Trinity Avenue, SW
Atlanta, GA 30334

Local Demographic Information
Ledger-Enquirer
P.O. Box 711
Columbus, GA 31994
Merry T. Tipton
404-324-5526

Hawaii

State Data Centers
Electronic Data Processing Division
Department of Budget and Finance
1151 Punchbowl Street
Honolulu, HI 96813
George Matsuo
808-548-4160

State Department of Planning &
Economic Development
P.O. Box 2359
Honolulu, HI 96804
Robert Schmitt/Bob Stanfield
808-548-3082
(Also provides state estimates, projec-
tions, and economic information.)

State Estimates
State Department of Health
P.O. Box 3378
Honolulu, HI 96801
Shigeo Tengan
808-548-5820

State & Local Economic Information
Research & Statistics
Department of Labor and Industrial
Relations
P.O. Box 3680
Honolulu, HI 96811

Fred Pang, Chief
808-548-7639

Vital Statistics
Research and Statistics Office
State Dept. of Health
P.O. Box 3378
Honolulu, HI 96801

Idaho

State Data Center
Idaho Department of Commerce
700 W. State Street
Boise, ID 83720
Alan Porter
208-334-2470

State & Local Economic Information
Economic Analysis Bureau
Division of Financial Management
Statehouse, Rm. 122
Boise, ID 83720
Derek Santos, Economist
208-334-2906
(Also provides state estimates.)

University Research Center
Boise State University
1910 University Drive
Boise, ID 83725
Chuck Skoro, Economist
208-385-1158
(Also provides state projections.)

Research & Analysis
Idaho Department of Employment
317 Main Street
Boise, ID 83735
James Day, Chief
208-334-2755

Department of Economics
The College of Idaho
Caldwell, ID 83605
W. Lamar Bollinger
208-459-5011

Center for Business Development &
Research
College of Business & Economics
University of Idaho
Moscow, ID 83843
Lawrence Merk, Director
208-885-6611

Vital Statistics
Idaho Cooperative Center for Health
Statistics
Vital Statistics - Health Statistics
450 W. State Street
c/o Statehouse
Boise, ID 83720
208-334-5988

Illinois

State Data Centers
Illinois State Data Center
Illinois Bureau of the Budget
William Stratton Bldg., Rm. 605
Springfield, IL 62706
Ann Geraci
217-782-3500

Division of Health Information &
Evaluation
Illinois Department of Public Health
535 West Jefferson St.
Springfield, IL 62761
Mark Flotow
217-785-5245
(Also provides state estimates.)

State & Local Economic Information
Office of Planning and Financial
Analysis
Illinois Bureau of the Budget
605 Stratton Office Building
Springfield, IL 62706
Cheng H. Chiang
217-782-3500
(Also provides state projections.)

Bureau of Economic & Business
Research
University of Illinois
1206 South Sixth Street
Champaign, IL 61820
Robert Resek, Director
217-333-2330

Department of Commerce & Community Affairs
Division of Research & Analysis
620 East Adams Street
Springfield, IL 62701
Wallace Biermann
217-782-1438

Vital Statistics
Office of Vital Records
State Dept. of Public Health
605 W. Jefferson Street
Springfield, IL 62702

Local Demographic Information
Chicago Tribune
435 N. Michigan Ave., Rm 1129
Chicago, IL 60611
Mary Lynn Owen
312-222-3184

The Pantagraph
301 Washington Street
P.O. Box 2907
Bloomington, IL 61701
Christopher B. Hanes
309-829-9411

Indiana

State Data Centers
Indiana State Library
Indiana State Data Center
140 North Senate Avenue
Indianapolis, IN 46204
Jeffery Barnett
317-232-3735

School of Business
Indiana Business Research Center
Indiana University
Bloomington, IN 47405
Morton J. Marcus, Director
812-335-5507
(Also provides state projections and
economic information.)

Division of Economic Analysis
Indiana Department of Commerce
1 North Capitol
Indianapolis, IN 46204
Charles A. Sim, Director
317-232-8959

State Estimates & Projections
Public Health Statistics
Indiana State Board of Health
1330 W. Michigan Street
Indianapolis, IN 46206
Robert A. Calhoun
317-633-0308

State & Local Economic Information
Office of Occupational Development
150 W. Market St., 7th floor
Indianapolis, IN 46204
Tamara Thompson
317-232-8542

Employment Security Division
10 North Senate Avenue
Indianapolis, IN 46204
Charles Mazza
317-633-4889

Vital Statistics
Division of Public Health Statistics
State Board of Health
1330 West Michigan Street
P.O. Box 1964
Indianapolis, IN 46206

Iowa

State Data Centers
Census Services
Iowa State University
318 East Hall
Ames, IA 50011
Willis Goudy
515-294-8337

State Library of Iowa
Historical Building
Des Moines, IA 50319
Pam Rees/Linda Mauer
515-281-4102

Census Data Center
Iowa Department of Social Services
Hoover State Office Building
Des Moines, IA 50319
Frank Poduskak
515)-281-4694

Academic Computing Services
University of Northern Iowa
11 Baker Hall
Cedar Falls, IA 50614
Jim Wolf
319-273-6815

Laboratory for Political Research
University of Iowa
321 Schaeffer Hall
Iowa City, IA 52242
Jim Grifhorst
319-353-3103

Center for Applied Social and Economic Statistics-IPAA
202 Old Main
Drake University
Des Moines, IA 50311
Bill Collins
515-271-2949

Ballou Library
Buena Vista College

Storm Lake, IA 50588
Barbara Palling
712-749-2127

State & Local Economic Information
Labor Market Information Unit
Iowa Department of Employment
Services
1000 East Grand Avenue
Des Moines, IA 50319
Mike Blank
515-281-8179

Institute for Economic Research
University of Iowa
Iowa City, IA 52242
Jerald Barnard
319-335-0835

Department of Management
Iowa State Capitol
Des Moines, IA 50319
Patrick D. Cavanaough
515-281-7077

Cooperative Extension Service
560 Heady Hall
Iowa State University
Ames, IA 50011
Daniel Otto
515-294-6147

Vital Statistics
Iowa Dept. of Public Health
Vital Records Section
Lucas State Office Building
Des Moines, IA 50319-0075

Kansas

State Data Centers
State Library
State Capitol Bldg., Rm. 343
Topeka, KS 66612
Marc Galbraith
913-296-3296

Division of the Budget
Room 152 E. Statehouse
Topeka, KS 66612
Mokhtee Ahmad
913-296-2436
(Also provides state estimates and
projections.)

Institute for Public Policy and Business
Research
607 Blake Hall
University of Kansas
Lawrence, KS 66045
Thelma Helyar
913-864-3701
(Also provides state and local economic
information.)

Population Research Laboratory
Department of Sociology
Kansas State University
Manhattan, KS 66506
Donald Adamchak
913-532-5984

Center for Urban Studies
Box 61
Wichita State University
Wichita, KS 67208
Mark Glaser
316-689-3737

State & Local Economic Information
Kansas Department of Commerce
400 S.W. 8th St. Suite 500
Topeka, KS 66603
A. Edwin Riemann
913-296-3481

Research & Analysis Section
Department of Human Resources
401 Topeka Avenue
Topeka, KS 66603
William H. Layes, Chief
913-296-5058

Vital Statistics
Bureau of Vital Statistics
Kansas State Dept. of
Health & Environment
900 S.W. Jackson
Topeka, KS 66612-1290

Kentucky

State Data Centers
State Data Center of Kentucky
Urban Studies Center
University of Louisville
Louisville, KY 40292
Michael Price
502-588-6626

Office for Policy & Management
State of Kentucky
Capitol Annex
Frankfort, KY 40601
William Hintze
502-564-7300

Department for Libraries & Archives
State Library Services Div.
300 Coffeetree Rd.
P.O. Box 537
Frankfort, KY 40602
James Nelson, State Librarian & Commissioner
502-875-7000

State Estimates & Projections
Population Studies
Urban Studies Center
University of Louisville
Louisville, KY 40292
Michael Price
502-588-6626

State & Local Economic Information
Kentucky Economic Information
System

Center for Business & Economic
Research
301 Mathews Building
University of Kentucky
Lexington, KY 40506-0047
Carol M. Straus
606-257-7675

Cabinet for Human Resources
275 East Main Street, 2nd Floor East
Frankfort, KY 40601
Ed Blackwell
502-564-7976

Vital Statistics
Office of Vital Statistics
Dept. for Health Services
275 East Main Street
Frankfort, KY 40621

Local Demographic Information
The Courier-Journal
Analysis & Research Department
525 West Broadway
Louisville, KY 40202
Mark R. Schneider
502-582-4351

Louisiana

State Data Centers
Louisiana State Planning Office
P.O. Box 44426
Baton Rouge, LA 70804
Karen Paterson
504-342-7410
(The main branch of the state data
center also provides state projections
and economic information.)

Division of Business and Economic
Research
University of New Orleans
New Orleans, LA 70148
Vincent Maruggi
504-286-6248
(Also provides state projections and
economic information.)

Division of Business Research
Louisiana Tech University
P.O. Box 10318
Ruston, LA 71272
Edward O'Boyle
318-257-3701

Louisiana State Library
Reference Department
P.O. Box 131
Baton Rouge, LA 70821
Blanche Cretini
504-324-4918

Experimental Statistics Department
173 Agriculture Administration Bldg.
Louisiana State University
Baton Rouge, LA 70803
George Tracy
504-388-8303

Research Division
College of Administration & Business
Louisiana Tech University
Box 10318 Tech Station
Ruston, LA 71272
James Robert Michael
318-257-3701
(Also provides state estimates and
economic information.)

State & Local Economic Information
College of Business Administration
Louisiana State University
8515 Youree Drive
Shreveport, LA 71115
John A. Marts, Associate Dean
318-865-7121

Division of Research and Development
College of Business Administration
Louisiana State University
Baton Rouge, LA 70803
David Johnson, Director
504-388-5830

Research & Statistics Department
Louisiana State Dept. of Labor

1001 North 23rd Street
P.O. Box 94094 - Capitol Station
Baton Rouge, LA 70804-9094
Oliver Robinson, Director
504-342-3141x321

Vital Statistics
Division of Vital Records
Office of Preventive &
Public Health Services
P.O. Box 60630
New Orleans, LA 70160

Maine

State Data Centers
Division of Economic Analysis and
Research
Maine Department of Labor
20 Union Street
Augusta, ME 04330
Raynold Fongemie/Jean Martin
207-289-2271
(The main branch of the state data
center also provides state and local
economic information.)

State Projections
State Planning Office
184 State Street
Augusta, ME 04333
Richard Sherwood
207-289-3261

State Estimates
Division of Data, Research & Vital
Statistics
Department of Human Services
Statehouse
Augusta, ME 04333
Dale E. Welch
207-289-3080

State & Local Economic Information
University of Maine
201 Alumni Hall
Orono, ME 04469

Gregory N. Brown, V.P. for
Research & Public Service
207-581-1504

Bureau of Taxation
Statehouse
Augusta, ME 04333
Edgar Miller, Economist
207-289-4135

Vital Statistics
Office of Vital Records
Human Services Building
Station 11
State House
Augusta, ME 04333

Local Demographic Information
Guy Gannett Pubishing Co.
P.O. Box 1460
Portland, ME 04104
Robert W. Cuzner, Director, Marketing
Research
207-775-5811

Maryland

State Data Centers
Department of State Planning
301 West Preston Street
Baltimore, MD 21201
Michel Lettre/Arthur Benjamin
301-383-5664
(The main branch of the state data
center also provides state projections
and economic information.)

Computer Science Center
University of Maryland
College Park, MD 20742
Glenn Ricart/John McNary
301-454-4323

State Estimates
Division of Statistics
and Population Estimates

Department of Health & Mental Hygiene
201 West Preston Street
Baltimore, MD 21201
Rose Marie Martin
301-225-5950

State & Local Economic Information
Maryland Department of Employment & Training
Department of Human Resources
1100 North Eutaw St., Rm. 518
Baltimore, MD 21201
Pat Arnold
301-932-5000

Bureau of Business & Economic Research
University of Maryland
Tydings Hall
College Park, MD 20742
John Cumberland
301-454-2303

Vital Statistics
Division of Vital Records
State Department of Health & Mental Hygiene
State Office Building
P.O. Box 13146
201 West Preston Street
Baltimore, MD 21203

Local Demographic Information
The Baltimore Sun
501 N. Calvert St.
Baltimore, MD 21278
John W. Cordes, Marketing & Research Manager
301-332-6245

Baltimore News American
South & Lombard
P.O. Box 1795
Baltimore, MD 21203
Allan B. Fleming, Marketing & Research Director
301-528-8312

Massachusetts

State Data Centers
Center for Massachusetts Data
Division of Community Services
Executive Office of Communities and Development
100 Cambridge St., Rm. 904
Boston, MA 02202
Charles McSweeney, Coordinator
617-727-7001
(The main branch of the state data center also provides state estimates and projections.)

Massachusetts Institute for Social and Economic Research
State Data Center Program
University of Massachusetts
117 Draper Hall
Amherst, MA 01003
Patricia Madson, Director
413-545-0176
(Also provides state estimates, projections, and economic information.)

State Estimates & Projections
Massachusetts Development Research Institute
University of Massachusetts
P.O. Box 11, Thompson Hall
Amherst, MA 01003
Stephen P. Coelen/Gordon F. Sutton
413-545-3460

State & Local Economic Information
Department of General Business & Finance
School of Management
University of Massachusetts
Amherst, MA 01003
Craig Moore
413-549-4930

Boston Redevelopment Authority
1 City Hall Square
Boston, MA 02201

Alexander Ganz
617-722-4300

Vital Statistics
Registry of Vital Records &Statistics
150 Tremont St., Rm. B-3
Boston, MA 02111

Michigan

State Data Centers
Michigan Information Center
Michigan Department of Management
and Budget
Office of Revenue & Tax Analysis
P.O. Box 30026
Lansing, MI 48909
Laurence S. Rosen
517-373-7910
(The main branch of the state data
center also provides state projections
and economic information.)

Office of Revenue & Tax Analysis
Department of Management & Budget
P.O. Box 30026
Lansing, MI 48909
Ching-li Wang
517-373-2697
(Also provides state estimates.)

MIMIC/CUS
Wayne State University
5229 Cass Avenue
Detroit, MI 48202
313-577-2180

Library of Michigan
Government Documents Division
P.O. Box 30007
Lansing, MI 48909
F. Anne Diamond
517-373-0640

State & Local Economic Information
Bureau of Business Research
School of Business Administration

Wayne State University
Detroit, MI 48202
David Verway
313-577-4213

Business Research Office
Department of Commerce
P.O. Box 30225
Lansing, MI 48909
Mark Murray
517-373-4600

Bureau of Research and Statistics
Michigan Employment Security
Commission
7310 Woodward Avenue
Detroit, MI 48202
Violetta Ogilvy
313-876-5447

Vital Statistics
Office of the State Registrar
& Center for Health Statistics
Michigan Dept. of Public Health
P.O. Box 30035
3423 North Logan Street
Lansing, MI 48909

Local Demographic Information
The Detroit News
Research Department
615 Lafayette Blvd.
Detroit, MI 48231
313-222-2223

Minnesota

State Data Centers
Minnesota Analysis and Planning
System
University of Minnesota-St. Paul
475 Coffey Hall
St. Paul, MN 55108
Phil Smith-Cunnien
612-624- 3283
(Also provides state and local economic
information.)

Office of Public Libraries and Interlibrary Cooperation
Minnesota Department of Education
440 Capitol Square Building
550 Cedar Street
St. Paul, MN 55101
Bill Asp
612-296-2821

State Estimates & Projections
State Planning Agency
300 Contennial Office Building
658 Cedar Street
St. Paul, MN 55155
R. Thomas Gillaspy
612-296-2557

State & Local Economic Information
Agri-Statistician
Box 7068
St. Paul, MN 55107
Carroll Rock
612-296-2230

State Planning Agency
300 Contennial Office Bldg.
658 Cedar Street
St. Paul, MN 55155
David Rademacher
612-297-3255

Bureau of Business and Economic Research
SBE Bldg., Rm. 150
University of Minnesota-Duluth
10 University Drive
Duluth, MN 55812
Donald N. Steinnes, Director
218-726-7298

Research and Statistics
Minnesota Department of Jobs and Training
390 N. Robert Street,
St. Paul, MN 55101
Med Chottepanda
612-296-6545

Vital Statistics
Minnesota Dept. of Health
Section of Vital Statistics
717 Delaware Street, SE
P.O. Box 9441
Minneapolis, MN 55440

Local Demographic Information
St. Paul Pioneer Press-Dispatch
345 Cedar Street
St. Paul, MN 55101
Diane Moser, Research Director
612-228-5305

Mississippi

State Data Centers
Center for Population Studies
The University of Mississippi
Bondurant Building, Rm. 3W
University, MS 38677
Michelle R. Plunk
601-232-7288
(The main branch of the state data center also provides state projections.)

Governor's Office of Federal-State Programs
Department of Community Development
301 W. Pearl Street
Jackson, MS 39203
Jeanie E. Smith/Glenn Duckworth
601-949-2219

State Estimates
Mississippi Research & Development Center
3825 Ridgewood Road
Jackson, MS 39211
Edward Ranck
601-982-6516
Philip Pepper
601-982-6408

State Projections
Mississippi Research & Development
Center
Economic Analysis Division
3825 Ridgewood Road
Jackson, MS 39211
Marilyn Moore
601-982-6314

State & Local Economic Information
Labor Market Information
Mississippi Employment Security
Commission
P.O. Box 1699
Jackson, MS 39215-1699
Raiford G. Crews, Chief
601-961-7424

Bureau of Business Research
School of Business Administration
University of Southern Mississippi
Southern Station, Box 94
Hattiesburg, MS 39401
D.C. Williams, Jr.
601-266-7247

College of Business & Industry
Mississippi State University
P.O. Drawer 5288
Mississippi State, MS 39762
J. William Rush
601-325-3817

Vital Statistics
Vital Records
State Board of Health
P.O. Box 1700
Jackson, MS 39215

Missouri

State Data Centers
Missouri State Library
2002 Missouri Blvd.
Jefferson City, MO 65101
Marlys Cresap Davis
314-751-0970

Urban Information Center
8001 Natural Bridge Road
University of Missouri
St. Louis, MO 63121
John G. Blodgett, Manager
314-553-6035

Missouri Office of Administration
Capitol Bldg, Rm. 129, Box 809
Jefferson City, MO 65102
Ryan Burson
314-751-2345
(Also provides state estimates, projec-
tions, and economic information.)

State & Local Economic Information
B and PA Research Center
University of Missouri
10 Professional Building
Columbia, MO 65211
Edward Robb
314-882-4805

Vital Statistics
Department of Health
Bureau of Health Data Analysis
P.O. Box 570
Jefferson City, MO 65102

Montana

State Data Centers
Census & Economic Information Center
Montana Department of Commerce
Capital Station, 1424 9th Ave.
Helena, MT 59620
Patricia Roberts
406-444-2896
(The main branch of the state data
center also provides state projections
and economic information.)

Bureau of Business & Economic
Research
University of Montana
Missoula, MT 59812
Larry Gianchetta, Acting Director

406-243-5113
(Also provides state estimates and
economic information.)

Center for Data Systems & Analysis
Office of the Vice President for
Research
Montana State University
Bozeman, MT 59717
Lee Faulkner
406-994-4481

Montana State Library
Capitol Station
Helena, MT 59620
Harold Chambers
406-449-3115

Vital Statistics
Bureau of Records & Statistics
State Department of Health and
Environmental Science
Helena, MT 59620

Nebraska

State Data Centers
Bureau of Business Research
College of Business Administration
University of Nebraska
Lincoln, NE 68588-0406
Donald Pursell
402-472-2334 & 2335
(The main branch of the state data
center also provides state projections
and economic information.)

Policy Research Office
P.O. Box 94601
State Capitol, Rm. 1319
Lincoln, NE 68509
Prem L. Bansal
402-471-2414

Nebraska Library Commission
1420 P Street

Lincoln, NE 68508
Rod Wagner/Lori Sailors
402-471-2045

Central Data Processing Division
Nebraska Department of Administrative
Services
306 State Capitol
Lincoln, NE 68509
Robert S. Wright/Skip Miller
402-471-2065

State Estimates
Nebraska Natural Resources Commis-
sion
P.O. Box 94876
Lincoln, NE 68509-4876
Mahendra Bansal
402-471-2081

State & Local Economic Information
Center for Applied Urban Research
University of Nebraska-Omaha
Omaha, NE 68182
Tim K. Himberger
402-554-8295

Nebraska Department of Revenue
Research Division
P.O. Box 94818
Lincoln, NE 68509
Gary B. Heinicke
402-471-2971

Department of Economic Development
P.O. Box 94666
301 Centennial Mall South
Lincoln, NE 68509
Stuart Miller, Director of Research
402-471-3783

Vital Statistics
Division of Health Data & Statistical
Research
State Department of Health
301 Centennial Mall South
P.O. Box 95007
Lincoln, NE 68509

Nevada

State Data Centers
Nevada State Library
Capitol Complex
401 North Carson
Carson City, NV 89710
Patricia Deadder
702-885-5160

Department of Data Processing
Capitol Complex
Blasdel Building, Room 304
Carson City, NV 89710
Bob Rigsby
702-885-5823

Office of Community Services
1100 East William St., Suite 117
Carson City, NV 89710
John Walker, Chief
702-885-4420
(Also provides state estimates and
projections.)

State Estimates
Bureau of Business & Economic
Research
College of Business Administration
University of Nevada-Reno
Reno, NV 89557
David Seymour
702-784-6877

State & Local Economic Information
Employment Security Research
500 East Third St.
Carson City, NV 89713
James Hanna, Chief
702-885-4550

Vital Statistics
Division of Health
Vital Statistics
Capitol Complex
Carson City, NV 89710

New Hampshire

State Data Centers
Office of State Planning
2 1/2 Beacon Street
Concord, NH 03301
Tom Duffy
603-271-2155
(The main branch of the state data
center also provides state estimates,
projections, and economic information.)

State Library
20 Park Street
Concord, NH 03301
John J. McCormick
603-271-2239

Office of Biometrics
COLSA UNH
James Hall, 3rd Floor
Durham, NH 03824
Owen Durgin
603-862-3930

State & Local Economic Information
Economic Research Office
Department of Research & Economic
Development
State of New Hampshire
Concord, NH 03301
George Bruno
603-271-2591

Vital Statistics
Bureau of Vital Records
Health & Welfare Building
Hazen Drive
Concord, NH 03301

New Jersey

State Data Centers
Office of Demographic & Economic
Analysis

Department of Labor
CN 388 - John Fitch Plaza
Trenton, NJ 08625-0388
Connie O. Hughes
609-984-2593
(The main branch of the state data
center also provides state and local
economic information.)

New Jersey State Library
185 West State Street
Trenton, NJ 08625-0520
Beverly Railsback
609-292-6220

Princeton-Rutgers Census Data Project
Computer Center
Princeton University
87 Prospect Avenue
Princeton, NJ 08544

Princeton-Rutgers Census Data Project
Center for Computer & Information
Services
Rutgers University
CCIS-Hill Center, Busch Campus
P.O. Box 879
Piscataway, NJ 08855-0879
Gertrude Lewis
201-932-2483

State Estimates & Projections
Office of Demographic & Economic
Analysis
Department of Labor, CN 388
Trenton, NJ 08625
Alfred Toizer
609-292-0076 & 0077

State & Local Economic Information
Center for Health Statistics
Dept. of Health, Rm. 405, CN-360
Trenton, NJ 08625
Henry A. Watson
609-984-6702

Department of Community Affairs
Division of Housing
South Broad & Front Sts.
CN-802
Trenton, NJ 08625
Lawrence W. Dolan
609-633-3889

Bureau of Economic Research
Rutgers University
State University of New Jersey
New Brunswick, NJ 08903
Paul Davidson
201-932-7451

Vital Statistics
Superior Court
Office of the Clerk
CN 971
Trenton, NJ 08625

Local Demographic Information
The Press & Sunday Press
1000 W. Washington Ave.
Pleasantville, NJ 08232
Susan S. Plage, Research Manager
609-272-1100, ext. 306

Asbury Park Press
3601 Highway 66, Box 1550
Neptune, NJ 07754
Marilyn Orloff, Research Manager
201-922-6000

New Mexico

State Data Centers
Economic Development and Tourism
Department
Bataan Memorial Building
Santa Fe, NM 87503
Ann Glover
505-827-6200

Bureau of Business & Economic
Research
University of New Mexico
Albuquerque, NM 87131
Lynn Bodin Wombold
505-277-2216
(Also provides state estimates, projec-
tions, and economic information.)

Center for Business Research &
Services
Box 3CR
New Mexico State University
Las Cruces, NM 88003
Kathleen Brook
505-646-1434
(Also provides state and local economic
information.)

New Mexico State Library
325 Don Gaspar Avenue
Santa Fe, NM 87503
Norma McCallan
505-827-3826

Vital Statistics
Vital Statistics Bureau
New Mexico Public Health Division
P.O. Box 968
Santa Fe, NM 87504-0968

New York

State Data Centers
New York Department of Economic
Development
One Commerce Plaza, Rm. 905
Albany, NY 12245
Robert Scardamalia
518-474-6005
(The main branch of the state data
center also provides state estimates,
projections, and economic information.)

Law & Social Sciences Unit
New York State Library
Cultural Education Center

Empire State Plaza
Albany, NY 12230
Elaine Scheerer
518-474-5128

Center for Governmental Rsch., Inc.
37 South Washington Street
Rochester, NY 14608
Melinda Whitbeck
716-325-6360

Capital District Regional Planning
Commission
214 Canal Square
Schenectady, NY 12305
Chanchin Chen
518-393-1715

Nelson A. Rockefeller Institute of
Government
411 State St.
Albany, NY 12203
Alison Chandler
518-472-1300

Central New York Regional Planning
and Development Board
90 Presidential Plaza, Suite 122
Syracuse, NY 13202
Paul Jasek
315-422-8276

CUNY Data Service
Graduate School and University Center
City University of New York
33 West 42nd Street
New York, NY 10036
Jonah Otelsberg
212-354-0640

Center for the Social Sciences
Columbia University
814 International Affairs Building
420 West 118th Street
New York, NY 10027
Walter Bourne
212-280-3038

Cornell Institute for Social and
Economic Research
323 Uris Hall
Cornell University
Ithaca, NY 14853
Ann S. Gray
607-255-4801

Dutchess County Department of
Planning
47 Cannon Street
Poughkeepsie, NY 12601
Carolyn Purcell
914-431-2480

New York Metropolitan Transportation
Council
One World Trade Center, 82nd Fl. E.
New York, NY 10048
Juliette Bergman
212-938-3352

Niagara Frontier Economic Development
Technical Assistance Center
Niagara County Community College
3111 Saunders Settlement Road
Sanborn, NY 14132
Bill Bordeau, Director
716-731-3271

Southern Tier West Regional Planning
& Development Board
465 Broad St.
Salamanca, NY 14779
Ginger Malak
716-945-5301

Center for Social and Demographic
Analysis
Social Science 376
State University of New York
Albany, NY 12222
Richard Alba, Director
518-442-4905

State University of NY at Buffalo
Regional Economic Assistance Center

305 Jacobs
Buffalo, NY 14260
Gail W. Parkinson
716-636-3240

Economic Development and Technical
Assistance Center
State University of New York
Plattsburgh, NY 12901
Gordon DeVries
518-564-2214

Population Division
Department of City Planning
22 Reade Street
New York, NY 10007
Evelyn Mann, Director
212-720-3434
(Also provides state and local economic
information.)

State & Local Economic Information
Program in Urban & Regional Studies
209 West Sibley Hall
Cornell University
Ithaca, NY 14853
Barclay Jones, Director
607-255-4331

Vital Statistics
Bureau of Vital Records
State Department of Health
Empire State Plaza
Tower Building
Albany, NY 12237

Bureau of Vital Records
Dept. of Health of NYC
125 Worth Street
New York, NY 10013

Marriage License Bureau
1780 Grand Concourse
Bronx, NY 10457

Office of the City Clerk
Marriage License Bureau

Municipal Building
210 Joralemon St.
Brooklyn, NY 11201

Marriage License Bureau
No. 1 Center Street
Municipal Building
New York, NY 10007

Marriage License Bureau
Queens Borough Hall
120-55 Queens Boulevard
Kew Gardens, NY 11424

Marriage License Bureau
Staten Island Borough Hall
St. George
Staten Island, NY 11201

Local Demographic Information
Newsday
Research Department
Long Island, NY 11747
Eileen Effrat
516-454-2401

Gannett Rochester Newspapers
55 Exchange Blvd.
Rochester, NY 14614-2001
Cindi A. Spezio, Research Analyst
716-258-2247

North Carolina

State Data Centers
North Carolina Office of State Budget
& Management
116 West Jones St.
Raleigh, NC 27603-8005
Allen J. Barwick
919-733-7061
(The main branch of the state data
center also provides state estimates,
projections, and economic information.)

State Library
North Carolina Department of Cultural
Resources
109 East Jones Street
Raleigh, NC 27611
Delores Porter
919-733-3343

Institute for Research in Social Science
University of North Carolina
Manning Hall 026A
Chapel Hill, NC 27514
Judy Poole
919-966-3346

State & Local Economic Information
Tax Research Division
North Carolina Department of Revenue
Raleigh, NC 27611
S. N. Underwood, Director
919-733-4549

Bureau of Employment Security
P.O. Box 25903
Raleigh, NC 27611
Donald Brande
919-733-2936

Department of Economics
University of North Carolina
Highway 49, Friday Bldg., Rm. 232
Charlotte, NC 28223
John Connaughton, Director

Bureau of Economic & Business
Research
John A. Walker College of Business
Appalachian State University
Boone, NC 28608
Rick Kirkpatrick, Director
704-262-2148

Center for Improving Mountain Living
Western Carolina University
Cullowhee, NC 28723
F. Merton Cregger, Director
704-227-7492

Vital Statistics
Department of Human Resources
Division of Health Services
Vital Records Branch
P.O. Box 2091
Raleigh, NC 27602

Local Demographic Information
The Charlotte Observer
600 S. Tryon Street
Charlotte, NC 28202
John Koslick, Marketing Research
Director
704-379-6342

The News and Observer
Publishing Company
P.O. Box 191
Raleigh, NC 27602
Robert L. Oney, Market Research
Director
919-829-4622

North Dakota

State Data Centers
North Dakota State Census Data Center
P.O. Box 5636
North Dakota State University
Fargo, ND 58105
Richard Rathge
701-237-8621 & 7980
(The main branch of the state data
center also provides state estimates,
projections, and economic information.)

Office of Intergovernmental Assistance
State Capitol, 14th Fl.
Bismarck, ND 58505
Jim Boyd
701-224-2094

Department of Geography
University of North Dakota
Grand Forks, ND 58202
Floyd Hickok
701-777-4593

North Dakota State Library
Liberty Memorial Building
Capitol Grounds
Bismarck, ND 58505
Doris Dougherty
701-224-4656

State & Local Economic Information
State Tax Commissioner
State Capitol
Bismarck, ND 58505
Katheryn L. Strombeck
701-224-2770

Bureau of Business & Economic
Research
University of North Dakota
290 Gamble Hall, Box 8255
Grand Forks, ND 58202
Bulent Uyar, Acting Director
701-777-2637

Research & Statistics
Job Service North Dakota
1000 East Divide, Box 1537
Bismarck, ND 58502
Tom Pederson, Chief
701-224-2868

Vital Statistics
Division of Vital Records
State Department of Health
Bismarck, ND 58505

Ohio

State Data Center
Ohio Data Users Center
Ohio Department of Development
Box 1001
Columbus, OH 43216
Barry J. Bennett, Manager
614-466-2115
(Also provides state estimates, projec-
tions, and economic information.)

State & Local Economic Information
Labor Market Information Division
Ohio Bureau of Employment Services
P.O. Box 1618
Columbus, OH 43216
Dixie Sommers, Director
614-481-5783

University of Toledo
Toledo Economic Information Systems
2801 West Bancroft St.
Toledo, OH 43606
Paul Kozlowski, Research Director
419-537-2687

University of Cincinnati
Mail Location #132
Cincinnati, OH 45221
Saul Pleeter, Director
513-475-5028

Vital Statistics
Division of Vital Statistics
Ohio Department of Health
G-20 Ohio Departments Bldg.
65 South Front St.
Columbus, OH 43266-0333

Local Demographic Information
The Cincinnati Enquirer
617 Vine Street
Cincinnati,OH 45202
Gerald T. Silvers, Research Director
513-369-1805

The Dispatch Printing Co.
34 South Third Street
Columbus, OH 43216
Doug Cavanaugh
614-461-5281

Oklahoma

State Data Centers
Oklahoma State Data Center
Department of Commerce

6601 Broadway Extension
Oklahoma City, OK 73116
Karen Selland, Director
405-843-9770
(The main branch of the state data
center also provides state projections
and economic information.)

Head of U.S. Documents
Oklahoma Department of Libraries
200 N.E. 18th Street
Oklahoma City, OK 73105
405-521-2502

State Estimates
Office of Economic Analysis
Oklahoma Employment Security
Commission
Will Rogers Memorial Office Building
Oklahoma City, OK 73105
Roger A. Jacks
405-557-7106
(Also provides state and local economic
information.)

State & Local Economic Information
Office of Business & Economic
Research
College of Business Administration
Oklahoma State University
Stillwater, OK 74078
Robert C. Dauffenbach, Director
405-624-5125

Center for Economic & Management
Research
University of Oklahoma
307 W. Brooks St., Rm. 4
Norman, OK 73019
Neil Dikeman, Jr.
405-325-2931

Vital Statistics
Vital Records Section
State Department of Health
Northeast 10th St. & Stonewall
P.O. Box 53551
Oklahoma City, OK 73152

Local Demographic Information
Oklahoma Publishing Co.
P.O. Box 25125
Oklahoma City, OK 73125
Clydette Womack, Marketing Research Manager
405-231-3577

Oregon

State Data Centers
Center for Population Research & Census
Portland State University
P.O. Box 751
Portland, OR 97207
Edward A. Schafer, Director
503-464-3922
(The main branch of the state data center also provides state estimates and projections.)

Bureau of Governmental Research & Service
University of Oregon
Hendricks Hall, Room 340
P.O. Box 3177
Eugene, OR 97403
Karen Seidel
503-686-5232

Oregon State Library
State Library Building
Salem, OR 97310
Craig Smith, Reference Supervisor
503-378-4277

State & Local Economic Information
Executive Department
State of Oregon
155 Cottage St., NE
Salem, OR 97310
Ann Hanus
503-378-3405

Department of Agric. & Res. Econ.
Oregon State University
Corvallis, OR 97331
Bruce Weber
503-754-2942

Library
Department of Economic Development
595 Cottage Street, NE
Salem, OR 97310
Peter Tryon
503-373-1227

Vital Statistics
Oregon State Health Division
Center for Health Statistics
P.O. Box 116
Portland, OR 97207

Pennsylvania

State Data Centers
Pennsylvania State Data Center
Institute of State & Regional Affairs
Pennsylvania State University at Harrisburg
The Capital College
Middletown, PA 17057
Robert W. Surridge, Director
717-948-6336
(The main branch of the state data center also provides state estimates, projections, and economic information.)

Department of Education
State Library of Pennsylvania
Forum Building
Harrisburg, PA 17120
John Geschwindt
717-787-2327

Office of Administration
Bureau of Management Services
903 Health and Welfare Bldg.

Harrisburg, PA 17120
Ray Kasper
717-787-9770

State & Local Economic Information
Division of Research
Pennsylvania State University
108 Business Administration, Bldg. II
University Park, PA 16802
Paul H. Rigby, Assoc. Dean
814-865-7669

Bureau of Statistics
Research & Planning
Commerce Department
469 Forum Bldg.
Harrisburg, PA 17120
Ron Kresge
717-787-4088

Research & Statistics
Pennsylvania Department of Labor &
Industry
7th & Forster Sts.
Harrisburg, PA 17121
Carl Thomas, Chief
717-787-3265

Vital Statistics
Division of Vital Statistics
State Department of Health
Central Building
101 S. Mercer Street
P.O. Box 1528
New Castle, PA 16103

Local Demographic Information
The Morning Call
P.O. Box 1260
Allentown, PA 18105
Linda C. Gibbard, Market Research
Supervisor
215-820-6729

The Times Leader
15 North Main Street
Wilkes-Barre, PA 18711

Gary R. Kromer, Director of Research
717-829-7100

Puerto Rico

Data Centers
Puerto Rico Planning Board
Minillas Government Center
North Bldg., Avenida De Diego
P.O. Box 41119
San Juan, PR 00940
Nolan Lopez Ramirez
809-723-6200, ext. 3876 & 2501
(The main branch of the data center also
provides estimates and projections.)

Department of Education
Carnegie Library
P.O. Box 759
Hato Rey, PR 00619
Carmen Martinez
809-724-1046

General Library
University of Puerto Rico
Mayaguez Campus
Post Street
Mayaguez, PR 00708
Grace Quinones-Seda, Director
809-832-4040

Rhode Island

State Data Centers
Rhode Island Statewide Planning
Program
265 Melrose St., Rm. 203
Providence, RI 02907
401-277-2656
(The main branch of the state data
center also provides state estimates and
projections.)

Rhode Island Department of State
Library Services

95 Davis Street
Providence, RI 02908
Frank Iacono
401-277-2726

Social Science Data Center
Department of Sociology
Brown University
Maxcy Hall, Angel St.
P.O. Box 1916
Providence, RI 02912
James Sakoda
401-863-2550

Rhode Island Dept. of Administration
Division of Planning
Office of Municipal Affairs
275 Westminster Mall
Providence, RI 02903
Paul M. Egan
401-277-2886

Rhode Island Health Services Rsch, Inc.
56 Pine Street
Providence, RI 02903
Roger Goulet
401-331-6105

State & Local Economic Information
Department of Employment Security
24 Mason Street
Providence, RI 02903
Raymond S. Mroz
401-277-3704

Department of Economic Development
7 Jackson Walkway
Providence, RI 02903
Vincent Harrington
401-277-2601

Vital Statistics
Division of Vital Records
State Department of Health
Rm. 101, Cannon Bldg.
75 Davis Street
Providence, RI 02908

South Carolina

State Data Centers
Division of Research & Statistics
State Budget & Control Board
Rembert Dennis Bldg., Rm. 337
1000 Assembly St.
Columbia, SC 29201
Bobby Bowers/Mike Macfarlane
803-734-3788
(The main branch of the state data
center also provides state estimates,
projections, and economic information.)

South Carolina State Library
P.O. Box 11469
Columbia, SC 29211
Mary Bostick, Documents Librarian
803-734-8666

State & Local Economic Information
Department of Business Administration
Baptist College at Charleston
P.O. Box 10087
Charleston, SC 29411
A.C. Flora, Jr.
803-797-4210

Division of Research
College of Business Administration
University of South Carolina
Columbia, SC 29208
R. C. Martin, Director
803-777-2510

Vital Statistics
Office of Vital Records & Public Health
Statistics
South Carolina Department of Health
& Environmental Control
2600 Bull Street
Columbia, SC 29201

South Dakota

State Data Centers
Business Research Bureau
School of Business
Patterson Hall, 414 E. Clark
University of South Dakota
Vermillion, SD 57069
DeVee Dykstra, Director
605-677-5287
(The main branch of the state data
center also provides state projections
and economic information.)

Documents Department
South Dakota State Library
800 Governors Dr.
Pierre, SD 57501-2294
Margaret Bezpaletz
605-773-3131

Center for Health Policy & Statistics
State Department of Health
523 E. Capitol Avenue
Pierre, SD 57501
Jan Smith
605-773-3693
(Also provides state estimates.)

Labor Market Information Center
South Dakota Department of Labor
P.O. Box 4730
Aberdeen, SD 57402-4730
Mary Susan Vickers, Director
605-622-2314
(Also provides state projections and
economic information.)

Census Data Center
Rural Sociology Department
South Dakota State University
Scobey Hall, 226
Brookings, SD 57006
Jim Satterlee, Director
605-688-4132

State & Local Economic Information
State Planning Bureau
Capitol Building
Pierre, SD 57501
Commissioner James Richardson
605-773-3661

Economics Department
South Dakota State University
Brookings, SD 57007
Ardelle Lundeen, Head
605-688-4141

Vital Statistics
State Department of Health
523 E. Capitol Avenue
Pierre, SD 57501

Tennessee

State Data Centers
Tennessee State Planning Office
John Sevier State Office Building
500 Charlott Avenue, Suite 309
Nashville, TN 37219
Charles Brown
615-741-1676
(The main branch of the state data
center also provides state estimates and
economic information.)

Center for Business & Economic
Research
University of Tennessee
Room 100, Glocker Hall
Knoxville, TN 37996-4170
David Hake
615-974-5441
(Also provides state projections and
economic information.)

State & Local Economic Information
Bureau of Business & Economic
Research

Memphis State University
Memphis, TN 38152
Paul Lowry
901-454-2281

Department of Economics & Finance
Middle Tennessee State University
Murfreesboro, TN 37132
R. N. Corcoran, Director
615-898-2528

Dept. of Employment Security
Research & Statistics Division
Cordell Hull Office Bldg., Rm. 519
436 Sixth Ave., North
Nashville, TN 37219
Joe Cummings, Director
615-741-2284

Vital Statistics
TN Center for Health Stats.
Department of Health & Environment
C2-242 Cordell Hull Bldg.
Nashville, TN 37219

Texas

State Data Centers
Texas State Data Center
P.O. Box 12728
Capitol Station
Austin, TX 78711
Susan Szaniszlo
512-472-5059
(The main branch of the state data
center also provides state estimates and
projections.)

Department of Rural Sociology
Texas A & M University
Special Services Building
College Station, TX 77843
Steve Murdock, Head
409-845-5332
(Also provides state estimates.)

Texas Natural Resources Information
System
P.O. Box 13087
Austin, TX 78711
Chas Palmer
512-463-8337

Texas State Library & Archive
Box 12927, Capitol Station
Austin, TX 78711
Bonnie Grobar
512-463-5455

State & Local Economic Information
Bureau of Business Research
University of Texas
P.O. Box 7459, University Station
Austin, TX 78713
Rita Wright
512-471-1616 or 5180

School of Business & Public Administration
University of Houston
2700 Bay Area Boulevard
Houston, TX 77058
Norman Weed
713-488-9420

Institute for Studies in Business
College of Business
University of Texas at San Antonio
San Antonio, TX 78285
Lynda Y. de la Vina, Director
512-691-4317

Water Uses, Projections, and Conserva-
tion Section
Texas Water Development Board
P.O. Box 13231, Capitol Station
Austin, TX 78711-3231
512-463-7940

Economic Research & Analysis
Texas Employment Commission
Tec Building

Austin, TX 78778
Horace Goodson, Chief
512-463-2326

Vital Statistics
Statistical Services Division
Bureau of Vital Statistics
Texas Department of Health
1100 West 49th Street
Austin, TX 78756-3191
Tom Pollard
512-458-7362

Utah

State Data Centers
Utah Office of Planning and Budget
State Capitol Bldg., Rm. 116
Salt Lake City, UT 84114
Brad Barber/Natalie Gochnour
801-538-1036
(The main branch of the state data
center also provides state estimates,
projections, and economic information.)

Bureau of Economic & Business
Research
Kendall D. Garff Bldg., Rm. 401
University of Utah
Salt Lake City, UT 84112
R. Thayne Robson
801-581-7274
(Also provides state estimates, projec-
tions, and economic information.)

Population Research Lab.
Department of Sociology
Utah State University
Logan, UT 84322-0730
William Stinner
801-750-1239

State & Local Economic Information
Utah Department of Employment
Security
P.O. Box 11249

Salt Lake City, UT 84147
Kenneth E. Jensen
801-533-2372
Larry K. Wardle, Director- Labor
Market Info. Services
801-533-2014
(Also a state data center.)

Vital Statistics
Bureau of Planning & Policy Analysis
Center for Health Information
288 North 1460 West, 4th Floor
P.O. Box16700
Salt Lake City, UT 84116-0700

Vermont

State Data Centers
Policy Research & Coordination Staff
Pavilion Office Building
109 State Street
Montpelier, VT 05602
Bernard Johnson/David Healy
802-828-3326
(The main branch of the state data
center also provides state and local
economic information.)

Center for Rural Studies
University of Vermont
25 Hills Building
Burlington, VT 05405
Fred Schmidt, Director
Tom Arnold
802-656-3021

Vermont Dept. of Libraries
111 State Street
Montpelier, VT 05602
Patricia Klinck, State Librarian
802-828-3265

Vermont Agency of Development &
Community Affairs
Pavilion Office Building
109 State Street

Montpelier, VT 05602
Jed Guertin
802-828-3211

State Estimates & Projections
Div. of Public Health Statistics
Vermont Department of Health
P.O. Box 70
Burlington, VT 05402
Lucy H. Gooding
802-863-7300

State & Local Economic Information
Policy & Information
Vermont Department of Employment &
Training
P.O. Box 488
Montpelier, VT 05602
Robert Warie, Director
802-229-0311

Vital Statistics
Vermont Department of Health
Division of Public Health Statistics
Box 70, 60 Main Street
Burlington, VT 05402

Virginia

State Data Centers
Department of Planning & Budget
445 Ninth Street Office Bldg.
P.O. Box 1422
Richmond, VA 23211
Larry Robinson/Donald Lillywhite
804-786-7844
(The main branch of the state data
center also provides state projections.)

Center for Public Service
University of Virginia
2015 Ivy Road, 4th Fl.
Charlottesville, VA 22903
James A. Norton, Director
804-971-2661
(Also provides state estimates and
economic information.)

Virginia State Library
11th Street at Capitol Square
Richmond, VA 23219-3491
Linda Morrissett
804-786-2175

State & Local Economic Information
Bureau of Business Research
School of Business Administration
College of William & Mary
Williamsburg, VA 23185
804-253-4493

School of Business Administration
Old Dominion University
Norfolk, VA 23508-8507
Richard Phillips
804-440-4713

Research & Analysis
Virginia Employment Commission
P.O. Box 1358
Richmond, VA 23211
Dewey T. Oakley
804-786-7496

Department of Economics
Virginia Commonwealth University
1015 Floyd Avenue
Richmond, VA 23284
Max Moszer
804-257-1593

Vital Statistics
Center for Health Statistics
State Department of Health
P.O. Box 1000
Richmond, VA 23208

Local Demographic Information
The Virginian Pilot & The Ledger Star
150 W. Brambleton Avenue
Norfolk, VA 23510
Lee Ann Dickson, Marketing Services
Manager
804-446-2439

VIRGIN ISLANDS

Data Center
Department of Commerce
P.O. Box 6400
Charlotte Amalie
St. Thomas, VI 00801
Richard Moore
809-774-8784, ext. 214

Washington

State Data Centers
Forecasting Division
Office of Financial Management
300 Insurance Bldg., MS AQ44
Olympia, WA 98504
Michael Knight
206-586-2504
(The main branch of the state data
center also provides state estimates and
economic information.)

Washington State Library
State Library Building
Olympia, WA 98504
Roderick G. Swartz/Ann Bregent
206-753-4027

Center for Social Science
Computation & Research
University of Washington
145 Savery, DK-45
Seattle, WA 98195
Dan Wancura
206-543-8110

Social and Economic Sciences Research
Center
Room 133, Wilson Hall
Washington State University
Pullman, WA 99164
Annabel Cook
509-335-1511

Demographic Research Laboratory
Department of Sociology
Western Washington University
Bellingham, WA 98225
Lucky M. Tedrow, Director
206-676-3617

State & Local Economic Information
Graduate School of Business Admini-
stration
DJ-10
University of Washington
Seattle, WA 98195
Philip Bourque, Business Economist
206-543-4484

Extension Service
203C Hulbert Hall
Washington State University
Pullman, WA 99164-6230
Gary Smith, Extension Economist
509-335-2852

Office of the Forecast Council
Department of Revenue
Evergreen Plaza Building
Olympia, WA 98504
Byron Angel

Vital Statistics
Vital Records
P.O. Box 9709, ET-11
Olympia, WA 98504-9709

Local Demographic Information
The Seattle Times
P.O. Box 70
Seattle, WA 98111
Carolyn S. Kelly, Marketing/New
Business Director
206-464-2319

Tacoma News-Tribune
P.O. Box 11000
Tacoma, WA 98411

Cathy J. Brewis, Director of Research
& Promotion
206-597-8563

Longview Publishing Company
c/o Daily Journal-American
P.O. Box 90130
Bellevue, WA 98009
Diana Lynne Tarlo, Corporate Research
Director
206-453-4293

West Virginia

State Data Center
Governor's Office of Community &
Industrial Development
Community Development Division
State Capitol Complex
Building 6, Room 553
Charleston, WV 25305
Mary C. Harless
304-348-4010
(The main branch of the state data
center also provides state estimates,
projections, and economic information.)

State Estimates & Projections
Applied Research, Evaluation &
Planning
Center for Extended & Continuing
Education
17 Knapp Hall
P.O. Box 6031
West Virginia University
Morgantown, WV 26506-6031
Sarah S. Etherton
304-293-4201

State & Local Economic Information
Bureau of Business Research
West Virginia University
P.O. Box 6025
Morgantown, WV 26506-6025
Tom S. Witt, Executive Director

304-293-5837 & 5839
(Also a branch of the state data center.)

State Tax Department & Center for
Economic Research
Research Division
West Wing Penthouse
Charleston, WV 25305
Alan L. Mierke
304-348-3478
(Also provides state projections.)

Vital Statistics
Office of Epidemiology & Health
Promotion
Health Statistics Center
State Department of Health
Charleston, WV 25305

Wisconsin

State Data Centers
Demographic Services Center
Department of Administration
101 South Webster
P.O. Box 7868
Madison, WI 53707-7868
Balkrishna Kale/Robert Naylor
608-266-1624/1927
(The main branch of the state data
center also provides state projections.)

Applied Population Laboratory
1450 Linden Drive
University of Wisconsin
Madison, WI 53706
Paul Voss, Senior Scientist
608-262-9526

State Estimates & Projections
Center for Health Statistics
Division of Health
Wisconsin Department of Health &
Social Service
P.O. Box 309

Madison, WI 53701
Henry Krebs
608-266-1920

State & Local Economic Information
Bureau of Labor Market Information
Department of Industry, Labor &
Human Relations
P.O. Box 7944
Madison, WI 53707
Hartley Jackson, Director
608-266-7034

External Relations
University of Wisconsin School of
Business
1155 Observatory Drive
Madison, WI 53706
William Strang, Associate Dean
608-262-1550

Department of Industry, Labor &
Human Relations
201 East Washington Avenue
P.O. Box 7944
Madison, WI 53707
Gerald Snow
608-266-0230

Bureau of Business and Economic
Research
University of Wisconsin
La Crosse, WI 54601
Gordon Sanford
608-785-8500

Vital Statistics
Center for Health Statistics
Wisconsin Division of Health
P.O. Box 309
Madison, WI 53701

Local Demographic Information
Milwaukee Journal-Sentinel
333 West State Street
Milwaukee, WI 53201
Charles Craft, Research Manager
414-224-2115

Wyoming

State Estimates
Institute of Policy Research
University of Wyoming
P.O. Box 3925, Univ. Station
Laramie, WY 82071
G. Fred Doll
307-766-5141
(Also provides state and local economic
information.)

State Projections
Department of Administration & Fiscal
Control
Division of Research & Statistics
302 Emerson Building
Cheyenne, WY 82002-0060
Steve Furtney/Phil Kiner
307-777-7221 or 7504
(Also provides state and local economic
information.)

State & Local Economic Information
Water Resources Research Institute
University of Wyoming
P.O. Box 3067, Univ. Station
Laramie, WY 82071
Clynn Phillips, Associate Director
307-766-2143

Employment Security Commission
ESC Building
100 West Midwest Avenue
P.O. Box 2760
Casper, WY 82602
Bill Davis
307-237-3646

Vital Statistics
Vital Records Services
Division of Health and Medical
Services
Hathaway Building
Cheyenne, WY 82002

NONPROFIT SOURCES OF DEMOGRAPHIC DATA

NONPROFIT ORGANIZATIONS ARE A DISPARATE GROUP. Some have detailed projections similar to those of private data companies; others conduct surveys and compile data on subjects that are not found elsewhere.

Academic Survey Research Organizations

There are scores of survey research organizations associated with universities around the country. For more information about where they are and what they offer contact Mary Spaeth, editor of **Survey Research**, a newsletter which reports on the activities of academic survey research organizations. She can be reached at the Survey Research Laboratory, University of Illinois, 1005 W. Nevada St., Urbana, IL 61801-3883.

Below is a short sample list of the current research that is being done by some of these organizations:

Massachusetts AIDS Study—Attitudes, Knowledge and At-Risk Behaviors
Center for Survey Research
University of Massachusetts—Boston
100 Arlington St.
Boston, MA 02116

Cross Cultural First Birth Study
Institute for Social Science Research
University of California at Los Angeles
9240 Bunche Hall, 405 Hilgard Ave.
Los Angeles, CA 90024

Determinants of Contraceptive Use by Adolescent Males
Institute for Survey Research
Temple University
1601 N. Broad St.
Philadelphia, PA 19122

Minority Female Single Parent Survey—Survey of Child Care Providers
Mathematica Policy Research
P.O. Box 2392
Princeton, NJ 08543

Health Cost Expenditures Survey
Minnesota Center for Survey Research
University of Minnesota
2122 Riverside Ave.
Minneapolis, MN 55454

Young Men's Survey of Life Experiences
NORC: A Social Science Research Center
University of Chicago
1155 E. 60th St.
Chicago, IL 60637

Farm Crisis Survey
Social and Economic Sciences Research Center
Washington State University
Wilson Hall #133
Pullman, WA 99164

Growing Up Chronically Ill Survey
Survey Research Center
University of California, Berkeley
2538 Channing Way
Berkeley, CA 94702

Psychosocial Aspects of Maternity Leave
Wisconsin Survey Research Laboratory
University of Wisconsin—Extension
Lowell Hall, 610 Langdon St.
Madison, WI 53703

THE CONFERENCE BOARD

Fabian Linden, Director
Consumer Research
Center
845 Third Avenue
New York, NY 10022
212-795-0900

Explaining consumer behavior to its corporate membership is the goal of the Conference Board's Consumer Research Center. The center analyzes the Census Bureau's annual demographic file, and cross-tabulates a number of variables, determining the total number of households, the average household size, aggregate income, and average household income for each cross-tab. Its reports are available only to members.

HOW TO JOIN THE CONFERENCE BOARD
Membership in the Consumer Research Center costs $1,950 a year for associates of The Conference Board, and $2,500 for nonassociates. Members receive all reports at no additional charge. The cost of association with the Conference Board varies according to the size of a firm and how much it uses the board's services.

WHAT YOU CAN GET FROM THE CONFERENCE BOARD

Consumer Market Guide

This statistical compendium is divided into 12 different subject chapters and contains over 300 statistical tabulations of information most frequently used by marketers.

How Consumers Spend Their Money

The center processes each computer tape from the Census Bureau's Consumer Expenditure Survey to get information on the most detailed products included in it. The results are published in a two-volume report showing spending on 463 product and service lines by the age of the householder, household size, age of children, type of household, earner composition, household income, education, occupation, region, race, and homeownership.

A Marketer's Guide to Discretionary Income

This report provides information on the amount of discretionary income buying power available for consumption and savings, after necessities are bought and taxes are paid.

Consumer Confidence Survey

This monthly newsletter reports the results of a panel survey of 5,000 representative households reported by age, income, and geographical region.

Consumer Market Watch

Another newsletter, it reports the most currently available data on income, employment, expenditures, prices, and the latest results from the Consumer Confidence Survey, with a consumer confidence index showing the present and expectations for the future, and a buying plans index. The confidence index also takes into account the inflation rate, interest rates, and stock prices.

INDUSTRY ASSOCIATIONS

There are thousands of trade associations in the U.S. which conduct surveys and other research for their respective industries. They are all listed, with addresses and phone numbers, in the **Encyclopedia of Associations**, a Gale Research Company publication which is available in the reference section of virtually any public library.

Below are just of few of the many trade associations that will provide information to researchers:

Finance/Insurance/   American Council of Life Insurance
Real Estate   1001 Pennsylvania Ave., NW
                         Washington, DC 20004-2505
                         202-624-2469

                         National Association of Realtors
                         430 N. Michigan Ave.
                         Chicago, IL 60611
                         312-329-8200

                         U.S. League of Savings Institutions
                         111 E. Wacker Dr.
                         Chicago, IL 60601
                         312-644-3100.

Food   Food Marketing Institute
                         1750 K St., NW
                         Washington, DC 20006
                         202-452-8444

                         National Restaurant Association
                         311 First St., NW
                         Washington, DC 20001
                         202-638-6100.

Media   Newspaper Advertising Bureau
                         1180 Ave. of the Americas
                         New York, NY 10036
                         212-921-5080.

                         Radio Advertising Bureau
                         304 Park Ave., S.
                         New York, NY 10010
                         212-254-4800

Television Bureau of Advertising
477 Madison Ave.
New York, NY 10022
212-486-1111.

Other

Photo Marketing Association International
3000 Picture Place
Jackson, MI 49201
517-788-8100.

Point-of-Purchase Advertising Institute (POPAI)
Two Executive Dr.
Fort Lee, NJ 07024
201-585-8400.

U.S. Travel Data Center
1113 21st St., NW
Washington, DC 20036
202-293-1040.

INSTITUTE FOR SOCIAL RESEARCH and the INTER-UNIVERSITY CONSORTIUM FOR POLITICAL AND SOCIAL RESEARCH (ICPSR)

University of Michigan
P.O. Box 1248
Ann Arbor, MI 48106

Founded in 1946, the Institute for Social Research is the largest university-based social research organization in the world. Most of its research projects are paid for by the government, but a few are undertaken for private corporations on the condition that the institute can publish the results.

The ICPSR, a branch of the Institute for Social Research, houses the largest American archive of social science data, incorporating data from the institute's own research, public surveys, the U.S. census, and research conducted at over 200 other universities. Its collection of machine-readable data includes census data, surveys of consumer attitudes, election returns, and other social science records. The staff does not do any programming, but will advise clients on how to use their local computing facilities. Although membership in the consortium is open only to educational institutions, the public at large may obtain data from ICPSR's archives at cost. Data are available on computer tape or online through the consortium's data network, **CDNET**.

WHAT YOU CAN GET FROM THE INSTITUTE FOR SOCIAL RESEARCH

Survey of Consumer Attitudes

This monthly trend report on consumer attitudes toward marketing conditions, business conditions and personal finance includes an index of consumer sentiment. It is available by subscription for $3,950 to $4,450. Selected data and customized analysis from it are also available upon request. For more information call Richard Curtin at 313-763-5224.

Panel Study of Income Dynamics

PSID provides detailed information about variations in families' economic fortunes. Unlike the Census Bureau's Current Population Survey, it interviews the same families year after year. Data from 1985 were available in 1988, both in print and on computer tape. For more information call Greg Duncan at 313-763-5186.

Study of American Families

A sample of women have participated in this study for over 15 years, producing data that show the relationship between fertility and marital stability, and the effects of such family characteristics as economic status, wife's labor force participation, and the changing patterns of sex roles. The latest interviews were conducted in 1987; however, only data through 1985 are currently available. For more information call Arland Thornton at 313-763-5015.

Monitoring the Future

This study is a nationwide survey of seniors from each new high school graduating class, beginning with the class of 1975, with annual follow-up surveys conducted for six years following graduation. The study topics include lifestyles, drug use, and plans for education, occupation, marriage, and parenthood. Data for 1975-1986 are available in printed form, a free monograph can be obtained from the Monitoring the Future Office at the Institute, and more detailed analyses are available for $40-$240 from the Institute's Book Sales department, Room 1213. For more information call Jerald Bachman at 313-763-5043.

American National Election Studies

This study, which compiles information from in-depth interviews with American adults, has been ongoing since

1948. It examines voter participation, partisanship, and trust in government. It also records current demographics of participants, including education, income, and occupation. Surveys are conducted every two years surrounding election years, and microdata are available from the ICPSR. For more information call Warren Miller or Santa Traugott at 313-763-0141.

CENTER FOR HUMAN RESOURCES RESEARCH

Gale James,
Coordinator
NLS Public Users
Office, Suite A
650 Ackerman Road,
Columbus, OH 43202
614-263-1682

Since 1966, the Department of Labor and Ohio State University have been following thousands of American men and women through the **National Longitudinal Surveys of Labor Market Experience**, which track individuals to learn how their lives are changing.

FOR MORE INFORMATION
The NLS Handbook is a comprehensive annual guide to the National Longitudinal Surveys of Labor Market Experience. It chronicles twenty years of NLS research and lists the publications, services, and data sets that can be obtained from the Center for Human Resources Research. For a free copy, contact the NLS Public Users' Office at the above address.

WHAT YOU CAN GET FROM THE CENTER FOR HUMAN RESOURCES RESEARCH

The data from the National Longitudinal Surveys are available in written reports and on computer tape for $250 to $300 per tape. To order call the NLS Public Users Office. Some of the reports which are available, which range in price from free to $1 per chapter, include:

Survey of Older Men   Studies the withdrawal from the labor force of civilian men who were ages 45 to 59 in 1966. Data are available for 1966 through 1983.

Survey of Mature Women   Followed civilian women who were 30 to 44 in 1967 to study the ages at which women who drop out of the labor force to have children typically return to work. Data are available for 1967 through 1984, and the 1986-87 interview results will be released in the summer of 1988.

Survey of Young Men

Followed civilian men who were ages 14 to 24 in 1966 to study the transition from school to work. Data are available for 1966 through 1981.

Survey of Young Women

Followed young women who were ages 14 to 24 in 1968 and, like the Survey of Young Men, studies the transition from school to work. Data are available for 1968 through 1983; 1985 and 1987 interview results were released in the spring of 1988.

National Longitudinal Survey of Youth (NLSY)

As the latter two groups began to age, a new panel was added which focused on young men and women who were ages 14 to 21 in 1979. This group includes military personnel plus an oversampling of Hispanics, blacks, and poor whites. Also available are NLYS Work History and NLYS Geocode data. Data are available for 1979 through 1986. The scheduled release date for 1987 NLSY interview results is fall 1988.

Children of the NLSY

Two new files follow the children of the NLSY and are based on 1986 interview data. **Child Assessment** looks at the children's development and home environment, while the **Merged Mother-Child Data** includes information on household composition, family employment, and child care. Additional NLSY public tape releases are scheduled for the fall of 1988.

POPLINE

Population Information Program
School of Hygiene and Public Health
Johns Hopkins Univ.
624 North Broadway
Baltimore, MD 21205
301-955-8200

Popline is the largest bibliographic demographic database in the world. It has items related to family planning and policy, as well as demography, fertility, education, migration and health care. Popline is updated monthly, and covers the period from 1970 to the present. It is available on-line through the National Library of Medicine's **MEDLARS** system.

HOW TO OPEN AN ONLINE ACCOUNT
Contact the National Library of Medicine, MEDLARS
Management Section, 8600 Rockville Pike, Bethesda, MD
20209; 301-496-6193.

THE POPULATION REFERENCE BUREAU (PRB)

777 14th St., NW, #800
Washington, DC 20005
202-639-8040

The PRB's goal is to increase public awareness of the facts
and implications of population trends. To that end, it
provides a number of publications and classroom-ready
teaching materials; training in population education; pol-
icy-oriented seminars, conferences, and briefings; demographic analyses for public policy; a research library; and
access to computerized databases.

HOW TO JOIN THE PRB
The annual fee ranges from $40 for an individual to $28 for
an educator, $20 for a student, and $50 for a library or nonprofit organization. Contact the PRB for details.

WHAT YOU CAN GET FROM THE PRB

Publications

The PRB puts out a wide variety of publications, ranging
from the inexpensive **Population Bulletins**, which are
often available with slides; to the monthly **Population
Today**, a magazine covering world population issues; to
the **U.S. Population Data Sheet**, an annual compilation of
population estimates, projections, and other useful data.

*Information Resource
Center*

This comprehensive research library is staffed with helpful
researchers and also has an online computerized bibliographic retrieval service to help clients with more in-depth
reference needs.

*Decision
Demographics*

A subsidiary of the PRB, Decision Demographics operates
on a fee-for-service basis and provides personalized, in-
depth data and analyses for corporate, governmental, or
individual clients seeking professional interpretation of
population trends.

THE POPULATION RESOURCE CENTER

Jane S. DeLung,
President
500 East 62nd Street
New York, NY 10017
212-888-2820

Nancy McConnell,
Director
110 Maryland Ave. NE
Washington, DC 20002
202-546-5030

WHAT YOU CAN GET FROM THE PRC
Using the services of the nation's leading authorities in demography, economics, and related fields, the Center organizes briefings, workshops, conferences, and commissioned research to analyze the relationship between demographic trends and key social and economic issues.

PRINCETON-RUTGERS CENSUS DATA PROJECT

Judith S. Rowe
Princeton University
Computer Center
87 Prospect Avenue
Princeton, NJ 08540
609-452-6052

Gertrude Lewis
Rutgers University
Center for Computer
and Info. Services
P.O. Box 879
Piscataway, NJ 08854
201-932-2483

WHAT YOU CAN GET FROM THE PRINCETON-RUTGERS CENSUS DATA PROJECT
This organization provides a full range of demographic data services, including printing data from computer tapes, merging files, creating custom diskettes for microcomputers, and producing computer graphics. They charge their commercial clients roughly the same prices a client would pay to use a private data company.

REGIONAL AND URBAN STUDIES INFORMATION CENTER (RUSTIC)

Mary L. Johnson
Building 4500 North
Mail Stop H32
Oak Ridge, TN 37831
615-576-8573

WHAT YOU CAN GET FROM RUSTIC
The Regional and Urban Studies Information Center has a varied collection of census and other historic demographic data. Its computerized socioeconomic database is one of the largest in the country, and includes tax, revenue sharing, mortality, attitude, and housing information. Because Oak Ridge is sponsored by federal agencies it only accepts private clients who can show that their data needs cannot be met elsewhere.

THE URBAN INSTITUTE

Thomas J. Espenshade
Director, Program in
Demographic Studies
2100 M. Street, NW
Washington, DC 20037
202-857-8547

The Urban Institute studies the social and economic problems of the nation's urban communities and government policies and programs designed to alleviate such problems.

FOR MORE INFORMATION
A catalog is available from the Institute.

WHAT YOU CAN GET FROM THE URBAN INSTITUTE

*The Demographic
Studies Program*

Emphasizes policy issues related to changing family and household demographics, international migration to the United States, and interrelations between population growth and economic development in developing countries.

*Dynamic Simulation
of Income Model*

DYNASIM projects the income and demographic characteristics of a nationwide sample of families. Unlike the Census Bureau's projections, which are only available aggregated, DYNASIM forecasts how demographic changes will affect individual families over time.

University Data Centers

The following university research and computing centers are members of the **National Clearinghouse for Census Data Services**, which means that they own tapes from the 1980 census (and will own them for the 1990 census) and will copy them, print tables, or extract data from them. These centers are primarily service bureaus, although some of them do more extensive research, both for themselves and for outside clients.

DELAWARE
Census and Data System
University of Delaware
Newark, DE 19716
Edward Ratledge
302-451-8406

Provides tape copies and printouts, file extracts, tabulations on disk, online access to data, and address matching/geocoding service.

FLORIDA
Census Access Program
University of Florida Libraries
Dept. of Reference and Bibliography
University of Florida
Gainesville, FL 32611
Margaret LeSourd, 904-392-0317
Ray Jones, 904-392-0361

Provides tape copies and printouts, file extracts, tabulations on disk, on-line access to data, microfiche printouts, analytical reports, and address matching/geocoding.

Census Group
Computing Center
Florida State University
Tallahassee, FL 32306
Lori McCraney, 904-644-4836

Provides tape copies and printouts, file extracts, tabulations on disk, and on-line access to data.

MAINE
Social Science Research Institute
164 College Avenue
Orono, ME 04473
Garrett Bozylinsky, 207-581-2555

Provides tape copies and printouts, file extracts, tabulations on disk, analytic reports, and training seminars.

MICHIGAN
Michigan State University
Computer Laboratory
East Lansing, MI 48824
Anders C. Johanson, 517-355-4684

Provides tape copies and printouts, file extracts, tabulations on disk, on-line access to data, analytic reports, address matching/geocoding, and training seminars.

MISSISSIPPI
Mississippi State University
Department of Sociology
P.O. Drawer C
Mississippi State, MS 39762
Ellen S. Bryant, 601-325-2495

Provides tape copies and printouts, file extracts, tabulations on disk, microfiche printouts, and analytic reports.

MISSOURI
University of Missouri-St. Louis
Computer Center
8001 Natural Bridge Road
St. Louis, MO 63121
John G. Blodgett, 314-553-5131

Provides tape copies and printouts, file extracts, analytic reports, address matching/geocoding, and training seminars.

NEW YORK
Columbia University
Center for the Social Sciences
814 International Affairs Building
420 West 118th Street
New York, NY 10027
Lauretta O'Dell, 212-280-3038

Provides tape printouts, file extracts, tabulations on disk, on-line access to data, microfiche copies and printouts, analytic reports, and training seminars.

CUNY Data Service, C.A.S.E.
Graduate School and Univ. Center
City University of New York
33 West 42nd Street
New York, NY 10036
Jonah Otelsberg, 212-354-0640 or
212-757-2188

Provides tape copies, file extracts, data and tabulation on disks, analytic reports, and training seminars.

User Services
University Computing Center
SUNY at Buffalo
4250 Ridge Lea Road
Amherst, NY 14226
Frank Rens, 716-831-1761/1771

Provides tape copies and printouts, file extracts, on-line access to data, microfiche copies and printouts, and address matching/geocoding.

OKLAHOMA
Oklahoma State University
University Computer Center
Mathematical Sciences Building 113
Stillwater, OK 74078
Eldean Bahm, 405-624-6301

Provides tape copies and printouts, file extracts, census map copies, and training seminars.

Rhode Island
Social Science Data Center
Brown University
Box 1916
Providence, RI 02912
James M. Sakoda, 401-863-2550

Provides tape copies and printouts, file extracts, tabulations from microdata files, and on-line access to data.

TENNESSEE
Memphis State University
Bureau of Business and
Economic Research
Memphis, TN 38152
Lew Alvarado, 901-454-2281

Provides tape copies and printouts, file extracts, microfiche copies, analytic reports, and training seminars.

WYOMING
University of Wyoming
Institute for Policy Research
P.O. Box 3925
Laramie, WY 82071
G. Fred Doll, 307-766-5141

Provides tape copies and printouts.

PRIVATE SOURCES of DEMOGRAPHIC DATA AND RELATED SERVICES

PRIVATE FIRMS ARE USUALLY THE BEST SOURCE for current estimates and projections of small geographic areas such as zip codes, counties, and even customized market areas. They also often combine demographic indicators with consumer media and purchase behavior. The turnaround time is usually immediate for this information. However, it can be expensive.

DEMOGRAPHIC DATA COMPANIES

Demographic data can range dramatically in price for what, to the uninformed, appears
to be the same set of numbers. The difference comes from what can be all-important
variations in how the numbers are calculated, customer service provided by the firm,
etc. Following are some questions that wise shoppers for data should ask before making
a purchase:

Five Tips on How to Shop for Data

1. Define your problem as precisely as possible.
If you know exactly what your problem is, you'll know exactly what you
need to solve it. And you won't waste any time or money pursuing information you don't need.

2. Find out when the firm was founded.
The older the firm the longer, and presumably the better, the track record.

3. Ask what their specialty is.
Some firms pride themselves on the quality of their county population projections, while others specialize in providing data geared to the needs of
financial analysts. Knowing what each firm concentrates on will help you sift
through their offerings.

4. Find out who prepares their data.
Is he or she a demographer, statistician, sociologist, etc.—the demographic
data industry is complex, so the more qualified the person who deals with the
data, the better off you will be.

5. Ask if customers are allowed to talk with the vendor's data experts.
Even if you're not a statistics whiz, you should understand how they arrived
at their numbers, which is especially important when you're buying estimates
and projections. (For more details about evaluating different vendors'
estimates and projections, see "Casting a Critical Eye" on page 49.)

MAJOR DEMOGRAPHIC FIRMS

These firms can offer you estimates, projections, databases, special reports, cluster analysis—if the need is there, one, and frequently all, of these firms can probably meet it.

CACI

Eric Cohen
Director of Advertising
Market Analysis Div.
8260 Willow Oaks
Corporate Drive
Fairfax, VA 22031
703-876-2342

Instant Demographics is CACI's database, which contains data for the current year and a five-year forecast, with 1980 historical data. The data are available online and through **SITELINE**, a call-in service for demographic, sales potential, and cluster analysis (ACORN) reports. The ACORN reports have been broken out for a variety of businesses, such as medical/health insurance, finance, investment services, eating out, etc. Maps displaying the data are also available.

MarketAmerica is a software program which combines CACI's demographic database and cluster system with integrated software for spreadsheet, business graphics, and map creation. It is especially useful for trade area analysis, direct marketing, competitive analysis, media planning, etc.

MarketAmerica's mapping program, **Atlas*Graphics**, which is produced by Strategic Locations Planning (see SLP's entry on page 182), can be purchased separately and integrated with either your or CACI's data.

CACI's cluster system is **ACORN** (A Classification Of Residential Neighborhoods), which categorizes 260,000 neighborhoods by 44 market types.

Finally, CACI produces the annual **Sourcebook of Demographics and Buying Power for Every ZIP Code in the USA**, and the **Sourcebook of Demographics and Buying Power for Every County in the USA**, desktop references that provide current-year estimates and five-year forecasts of key demographic characteristics. Information from CACI's cluster system about purchasing potential is included. Both books are also available on disk and tape.

CLARITAS

Dick Raines
Marketing Director
201 N. Union St.
Alexandria, VA 22314
703-683-8300

Claritas has a cluster system called **PRIZM**, which classifies all U.S. households into 40 neighborhood types. Additionally, they have a cluster system specifically for financial marketers called **P$YCLE**, which is based on information about consumers' household income, work/retirement status, business- and home-owner status, age, and income-producing assets.

   Claritas also produces **COMPASS**, a PC system which combines customers' company records, data from their PRIZM and P$YCLE cluster systems, and cartographic data, enabling users to identify and rank markets and create maps.

DONNELLEY MARKETING INFORMATION SYSTEMS

Stephen Speier
Director of Marketing
70 Seaview Ave.
Stamford, CT 06902
800-527-DMIS

Donnelley has a wide range of products and services, including:
• **American Profile,** current-year estimates and five-year projections for key demographic variables such as age, sex, households, etc.
• **Market Potential,** current-year data on potential sales volume for 21 types of retail stores.
• **GraphicProfile,** demographics in map form.
• **TargetScan,** a computerized search for areas that match specific demographic profiles.
• **ZIProfile,** current-year estimates, five-year projections, and other demographic data for zip codes and carrier routes.
• **ZIP Code Guide,** a directory with current-year population, household, and median household income data by zip code.
• **ClusterPlus,** Donnelley's cluster analysis system which groups geographic areas into 47 lifestyle segments.
• **Shopping CenterProfile,** data on 24,000 shopping centers around the country.
• **Donnelley Diagnostics,** data on the healthcare industry.
• **Income by Age,** cross-tabulations based on estimates of household income by age of household head.
• **CONQUEST,** market analysis software.

MARKET STATISTICS

Robert M. Katz
Sr. Vice President
633 Third Ave.
New York, NY 10017
212-986-4800

Known for its attention to methodological detail, Market Statistics provides estimates and projections through 2007 on population, income, and retail sales. They also produce the **Merchandise Line Report**, which contains product specific information based on the 1982 Census of Retail Trade.

The firm also provides 1987 employment data by SIC code, and key demographic and economic variables by zip code

Market Statistics' software program, **Your Marketing Consultant–Consumer**, allows users to search, select, and rank 39 demographic, economic, and retail sales variables. **Your Marketing Consultant–Business-to-Business** lets users perform the same functions with a variety of market types and data variables, including establishment, employment, and occupation data.

Finally, Market Statistics produces the data for the annual **Survey of Buying Power** and the **Data Service**, highly-respected publications which detail the population, income, retail sales, buying power figures, and much more for virtually all geographies, including TV and newspaper markets.

NATIONAL DECISION SYSTEMS

Nancy Belford,
Head of Marketing
539 Encinitas Blvd.
Encinitas, CA 92024
619-942-7000

NDS produces **Infomark**, a PC system that has six databases on a 12-inch optical disk, which is the equivalent of 3,000 floppy disks. The databases contain demographic information, profiles from their cluster system, data on business and daytime population, product and media usage, specific industries, consumer expenditures, geographic references, and map coordinates. Customers can also add their own data to the system. Infomark generates maps and tabular reports, and operates on an upgraded IBM/AT/XT or IBM Personal System/2.

NDS also provides a line of market analysis/site selection tools, and a cluster system called **VISION**, which classifies every U.S. household into one of 48 market segments. An extension of VISION is **FutureVISION**, a database which incorporates mobility data into their cluster system to forecast where specified markets will be three to ten years from now.

The firm provides a complete line of reports on demographics, business and competition, daytime population and employment, consumer expenditures, consumer demand for specific products and services, shopping centers, and such specific industries as restaurants and financial institutions.

NATIONAL PLANNING DATA CORPORATION

(Call for the name of the sales representative nearest you.)
P.O. Box 610
Ithaca, NY 14851-0610
607-273-8208

NPDC provides current-year estimates and five-year projections for a wide variety of subjects and geographic areas, with special reports available on the 55+ market, the healthcare market in metropolitan areas, the labor force, and consumer purchasing for detailed product categories. The firm has several databases which combine their estimates and projections with data from the Summary Tape Files and special tabulations of the 1980 census: the **Yellow Pages Data System**, which adds business information by SIC codes, and the **MAX Online Demographic System**, which has additional data for the 55+ population; a special feature of MAX is that you can add your own data to the file.

NPDC also provides extensive data on business patterns for counties and zip codes, both in print and on tape.

Their thematic mapping package is called **MAXpc MapAnalyst**, and it downloads data from the MAX database and produces presentation-quality maps using five data classification methods. The program works on an IBM-PC or compatible. NPDC offers several training seminars on using their MAX and MapAnalyst systems; call for details about dates and locations.

URBAN DECISION SYSTEMS

Elliott Steinberg
Sales Manager
2040 Armacost Avenue
Los Angeles, CA 90025
213-820-8931

One of UDS's specialties is its **Shopping Center Reports**, which provide demographic data—daytime population, occupation, income, etc.—on the potential customers of shopping centers in user-defined trade areas. Also available from UDS are **Retail Potential Reports**, which estimate consumer spending potential for a broad range of stores, shopping centers, and merchandise lines; **Income and Demographic Trends Reports**, and **Population Benchmark Reports**, which compare key demographic indicators for any three areas. New reports from UDS include **Daytime Marketplace**, **Retail Sales & Competition**, and **Business Profile**.

In the area of mapping, UDS produces **COLORSITE Grid Images**, which display data variables through a network of equal-sized squares colored according to the density of the selected variable. They are available for neighborhoods on up to states and include major highways, county boundaries, and other orientation aids.

DATA SPECIALISTS

These firms, smaller than the major demographic data vendors, specialize in providing certain types of data, or data on a particular market.

CENTER FOR CONTINUING STUDY OF THE CALIFORNIA ECONOMY

Aviva Bernstein
Marketing Director
610 University Avenue
Palo Alto, CA 94301
415-321-8550

SPECIALTY
The California market

CCSCE specializes in economic and demographic studies for public and private sector clients. Out of these projects come a variety of reports on such topics as household income and spending power, population by ethnic group and age, etc. They conduct seminars and management briefings on the impact of national trends on California, the outlook for the California economy, and trends in customers' market areas, and are well-known for their projections of California economic and population growth.

COM KEY SYSTEMS, INC.

Bernie Peterson
1411 W. Alabama,
Suite 200
Houston, TX 77006
713-522-1915

SPECIALTY
The Houston market

Com Key has a database called **Key-Site**, which generates reports about the demographics of the Houston market: estimates, projections, population profiles, etc. Geographic selections include circles around a street address or intersection, rectangles, zip code areas, census tracts, and customer-defined areas.

DEMO-DETAIL

Richard Irwin, Director
2303 Apple Hill Road
Alexandria, VA 22308
703-780-9563

SPECIALTY
County estimates

Demo-Detail provides estimates by age, sex, and race for all U.S. counties for 1980 through July 1, 1986. You can get them in reports, or on a disk (PC DOS 2.1), and the national file is available on tape.

INSTANT RECALL

David Shaw
P.O. Box 30134
Bethesda, MD 20814
301-530-0898

SPECIALTY
Data from federal
agencies and nonprofit
organizations

Instant Recall's database is loaded with statistics from the Census Bureau and an intriguing combination of 11 other agencies, including the National Center for Health Statistics, American Dental and Nurses Associations, Health Care Financing Administration, Social Security Administration, FBI, Bureau of Labor Statistics, Bureau of Economic Analysis, Federal Deposit Insurance Corporation, Federal Home Loan Bank Board, and the Elections Research Center. When you buy the system, you get a general data disk with basic variables and can then purchase special disks with detailed variables for certain subjects, such as health, income, construction, etc. You can also add your own data. The numbers are displayed in maps, graphs, and tables, and updates are available. It operates on an IBM PC or compatible, with 128K RAM and PC-DOS/MS-DOS.

POPULATION RESEARCH SERVICE

Bryan Lambeth
P.O. Box 181032
Austin, TX 78718
512-836-7888

SPECIALTY
Estimates

Population Research Service provides quarterly-updated estimates for percent growth, net growth, current population, and housing for all major U.S. cities and metro areas; available in printed reports and on diskettes.

SLATER HALL INFORMATION PRODUCTS

Courtenay Slater
Chairman of the Board
1522 K St., NW
Washington, DC 20005
303-682-1350

SPECIALTY
Economic databases

Slater Hall provides data on compact optical discs, which hold huge databases—one disk is the equivalent of 1,500 floppy disks, or about 250,000 printed pages. They currently have four disks available: **1982 Census of Agriculture**; **Business Indicators**, which is updated monthly and includes the National Income and Product Account from 1929 to the present, plus the economic time series from the Survey of Current Business, and income and employment by industry for every state; **County Statistics**, the Census Bureau's new COSTATS file; and **Population Statistics**. The disks come with a retrieval program called Searcher, and they operate on an IBM-PC or compatible, with at least 512K RAM, and a CD-ROM reader with driver.

WESTERN ECONOMIC RESEARCH COMPANY, INC.

C. Michael Long
Vice President
15910 Ventura Blvd.,
Suite A-8
Encino, CA 91436-2802
818-981-9762

SPECIALTY
Estimates and census-
based maps and reports

WERC provides annually-updated, prepackaged estimates of population, households, age, income, and total employment for states and zip codes. Their maps and reports are based on the 1980 census and are available on a wide range of subjects and geographies.

FORECASTING FIRMS

When buying forecasts, which are virtually the same thing as projections, it is important to ask how they are prepared, how often they're updated, how far into the future they forecast, and the geographic regions they cover.

ANALYSIS AND FORECASTING, INC.

John R. Pitkin, President
P.O. Box 415
Cambridge, MA 02138
617-491-8171

SPECIALTY
Households and housing

A&F provides estimates, projections, and reports on households and housing for counties, MSAs, states, regions, and the nation. Their data cover such details as size and type of household, presence of children, number of earners, and type of housing. In collaboration with Cambridge Systematics, A&F also specializes in the implications of future population trends for business and government.

DATA RESOURCES INC.

(Call to get the name of the sales representative nearest you.)
24 Hartwell Avenue
Lexington, MA 02173
617-863-5100

SPECIALTY
Historical and forecast databases

DRI has more than 125 databases covering a broad range of financial, industrial, economic, and international topics. Accessible by PC, timesharing, or directly from mainframe to mainframe, they include:

• **Consumer Markets Forecast**, which examines personal consumption expenditures for a variety of durable and nondurable consumption categories, discretionary income, retail sales, and nondurable goods stores.

• **County Forecast**, which provides data on employment, income, population, births, deaths, migration, households, etc.

• **Metropolitan Area Forecast**, which has data on employment, personal income, population, single and multi-family housing permits, and labor market indicators for 313 metro areas.

• **Regional Model Forecast**—data on industry employment and production, personal and disposable income, prices and wages, housing starts, population and households, unemployment, retail sales, etc., in regions and states.

THE FUTURES GROUP

Cornelia Sheridan
Hanbury, Manager,
Consumer Studies
76 Eastern Blvd.
Glastonbury, CT
06033-1264
203-633-3501

SPECIALTY
Consumer purchasing
patterns

The Futures Group analyzes and forecasts consumer behavior—spending patterns, budget choices, saving, bor-
rowing—ten years into the future, and their data are available through two Consumer Markets reports: **Consumer
Purchasing Patterns**, monthly analytical reports focusing
on trends in specific consumer markets, and **Consumer
Purchasing Power Trends for Key Customer
Segments**, twice-a-year analysis and projections of the
purchasing power of major market segments, with income
distribution in both current dollars and inflation-adjusted
dollars broken out by age group and type of household.

The Futures Group also produces **StatPlan III**, statistical software with forecasting capability and graphical
display which runs on an IBM PC, XT, AT, COMPAQ, or
compatible with 256K RAM and one disk drive.

NPA DATA SERVICES, INC.

Nestor E. Terleckyj
1616 P Street, NW,
Suite 400
Washington, DC 20036
202-265-7685

SPECIALTY
Projections

NPA produces the annually-updated **Regional Economic
Projections Series**, or REPS, which projects a range of
subjects, including employment, earnings, and personal
income by regions, states, metropolitan areas, and counties. The data are available in written reports, printouts,
diskettes (for IBM PC and Apple Macintosh), tapes, and
online.

THE WEFA GROUP
(Wharton Econometric Forecasting Associates)

Doug Todd
Director of Marketing
150 Monument Rd.
Bala Cynwyd, PA
19004
800-322-9332

SPECIALTY
Econometric
forecasting

The WEFA Group, known for in-depth economic and
consulting services, provides the **Long-Term Service**
which examines demographic shifts, technology developments, and other changes expected to occur over the next
ten years, information which is especially useful for strategic planning. They also provide an array of consulting
services, including alternative scenarios, product-line
forecasts, and market-potential assessment.

WOODS & POOLE ECONOMICS

Sallie L. Poole, Vice
President, Marketing
1794 Columbia Rd. NW
Washington, DC 20009
202-332-7111

SPECIALTY
County-level forecasts

Woods and Poole's individual analyses of every county
and MSA in the U.S. includes forecasts through 2010 for
more than 300 economic and demographic variables, including employment by industry, earnings by industry,
personal income by source, household data and population
by age, sex and race. The data, which are updated each
year, are available in printed reports, and on disk and tape.
The firm also consults with clients and provides custom
forecasts.

COMPUTER MAPPING FIRMS

Maps generated by computers combine geography with demographic information and
the user's company data. Their advantage is that they can display several variables at
once and quickly point out areas where certain groups of consumers do—and don't—
live.

Questions You Should Ask About
Computer Mapping by Marci L. Belcher, MPSI Systems, Inc.

1. Do you need a mainframe or a microcomputer-based mapping system?
Large, centralized companies should consider mainframe programs. They
store and process large data files, usually offer features supporting more
complex problem solving, and can be shared by multiple users. Small
organizations will find that microcomputer-based mapping systems offer
many of the capabilities of the mainframe packages, but at a much lower cost.

*2. Does the system manage information linked to varied types of
geography?*
All mapping programs manage demographic information by census tract and
zip code, but the better ones can also manage information such as sales
performance by location and traffic counts by street network.

3. Can you use multiple variables?
Better systems allow you to use relational and logical operators to ask
questions using a number of variables. The map shows only the geographic
areas that satisfy the specified condition. Other programs allow you to
identify only one or two variables which are displayed for all areas.

4. Does the system integrate data from disparate types of geography?
Programs with this feature allow you to use data referenced by zip code with data referenced by census tract, eliminating the need to geocode to a common geographic type.

5. Does the system perform density calculations?
Mapping programs that display only raw counts or percentages can lead to misinterpretation. The best systems perform density calculations that show you, for example, how concentrated an area's population is.

6. Does it zoom?
This is important if you're using maps to study sites or street networks that are close to one another. Some zooms only blow up a picture; the better ones will show you greater geographic detail.

7. How accurate is the system's cartography?
The most advanced mapping products display longitude and latitude coordinates and a scale that allows you to calculate exact distances between locations.

8. Can you report information and how flexibly?
Programs that offer reporting eliminate the need to transfer data to other software packages for calculation. Some programs that offer reporting, however, print out only preselected data in a standardized format.

9. How good is the quality of details on the finished map?
Different systems have different types of hatching, cross-hatching, symbols and patterns, texts, and legend boxes. Check them out.

10. How easy is the system to use?
A mapping program should include on-line help, fully prompted input screens, and an English-like command language that requires little or no familiarity with programming languages. You should be able to save, recall, and edit your queries and plotting specifications.

11. How good are the vendor's geographic files?
Some companies specialize in providing highly detailed map files that include features such as cities, parks, airports, lakes, rivers, bridges, and transportation networks. This eliminates the need to use base maps for further reference.

12. Can you digitize?
The mapping products that include digitizing will allow you to add or change map features. This is particularly useful if you're studying markets that are rapidly changing.

13. How easy is it to add, delete, and modify data in the system?
As more information becomes available and other information becomes outdated, it is important that you be able to easily modify your databases.

14. How supportive is the company?
The company you buy a complex mapping system from should provide
training, installation, testing, tutorials, system documentation, and toll-free
telephone assistance. Some companies also offer enhanced versions of
software and data through a licensing agreement, helping you stay up to date.

—Reprinted from American Demographics magazine.

MAPPING SOFTWARE

DATAMAP, INC.

Richard M. Byers
National Sales Manager
7176 Shady Oak Rd.
Eden Prairie, MN
55344
612-941-0900

Datamap produces **CAM-1**, a software program for direct
mail targeting and site and territory analysis. It retrieves
and presents the census demographics of carrier routes for
316 MSAs. It runs on an IBM XT, AT or compatible, a
graphics adapter, a 10 megabyte hard disk, and 512K
memory. Using its Postal Carrier Route and Census Block
Group databases, Datamap can also produce maps, tabular
data, or tapes to analyze the populations of areas as small
as one-tenth of a mile increments or fewer than 300 households.

ENVIRONMENTAL SYSTEMS RESEARCH INSTITUTE (ESRI)

Karen Hurlbut
380 New York St.
Redlands, CA 92373
714-793-2853

ESRI provides **ARC/INFO**, a sophisticated software system for managing geographic information and producing
high quality maps. The system combines geographic
analysis and modeling capabilities with an interactive
system for entry, management, and computer display of the
data. It is especially useful for land records and property
management, urban and regional land use planning, thematic mapping, and environmental and natural resource
management. ARC/INFO operates on 32-bit mini and
mainframe computers and has recently been released on
the IBM PC/AT. ESRI provides a range of other services,
including database design, mapping, digitizing, and consulting.

MODERN BUSINESS APPLICATIONS, INC.

Maria Hosford
Manager Marketing
& Sales
67 GAR Highway
Somerset, MA 02725
617-678-6577

MBA produces **Select.Site**, a PC system in which you call up a selected MSA on the screen, draw any size or shape trade area on it, and immediately obtain a demographic profile for the area you've indicated. The program has over 1000 variables—age, income, housing value, ethnic group, sex, etc.—with 1980 actuals, current-year estimates, and five-year projections for most of them. Also included are an intriguing list of market potential indices such as vehicles per household, radio listeners, TV viewers, restaurant sales by type of meal, and number of mufflers installed. Purchasers can buy all the variables or just the ones they're interested in, for any MSA. Select.Site, which gets its data from CACI (see page 167), operates on an IBM PC/XT or AT, or compatible, with color monitor.

MPSI SYSTEMS, INC.

Joe Perrault,
Sr. Manager,
Marketing/Planning
8282 S. Memorial Dr.
Tulsa, OK 74133
918-250-9611

MPSI, an international firm which specializes in computer software and information services, has a software system of special interest to marketers called GIS, or **Geographic Information System**. It links data to geography—from counties down to road networks—and provides the results in color maps and tabular reports. Your data can be combined with MPSI's databases on retail outlet information, specialized demographics, land-use data, and traffic counts, and MPSI will also generate geographic files for your trade areas and distribution networks.

SAMMAMISH DATA SYSTEMS, INC.

Richard Schweitzer
President
1813 - 130th Ave., NE,
Suite 218
Bellevue, WA 98005
206-867-1485

Sammamish provides a software system called **GeoSight** which integrates mapping and database management systems. It combines statistical and demographic databases (yours and/or those of any of the major data companies) with its mapping capabilities to display and analyze data associated with geographical areas. The boundary files are purchased separately, as is the software that allows you to turn the mapped data into tabular reports. GeoSight operates on an IBM AT, PS/2 Model 50, or a Compaq 386 (or equivalent), with an 80287 math coprocessor and an EGA graphics card.

Sammamish Data also produces **DIDS**, a PC mapping program, and **QuickMap**, an integrated subset of the DIDS system, designed for people with fairly basic mapping needs.

STRATEGIC LOCATIONS PLANNING

Stephen Poizner
President
4030 Moorpark Ave.,
Suite 123
San Jose, CA 95117
408-985-7400

SLP provides **Atlas*Graphics**, a software program that maps census geography, zip codes, and market areas; users can enter their own data and create customized boundary files. (Atlas*Graphics is also part of CACI's Market America software program, described on page 167.) A new product from SLP is the **Laser Pak**, a laser disk designed to be used with Atlas*Graphics which contains virtually all U.S. boundary and data files.

MAP PRODUCTION

INTELLIGENT CHARTING, INC.

Valerie Griffin
National Sales Manager
975 Convery Blvd.
Perth Amboy, NJ 08861
201-826-9292

Intelligent Charting creates customized computer-generated maps, and will analyze the maps and consult with you on what business decisions you should make based on the information revealed by them. You submit the categories you want mapped on a tape, diskette, tabular report, or handwritten letter, and they will produce the maps according to a wide range of area boundaries such as zip codes, counties, states, Yellow Pages, custom territories, etc.

RAND MCNALLY

Mike Kelly (THEMAP)
Dawn Checchin
(RANDATA and
publications)
8255 N. Central Park
Ave.
Skokie, IL 60076-2970
800-332-RAND
312-673-9100
in Illinois

Rand McNally, famous for its atlases, provides customized computer-generated maps through its **THEMAP** service. You can either provide the data yourself or choose from Rand McNally's data categories, which include SIC codes at the zip code level, and such demographic variables as population, age, income, buying power, and retail sales by county or zip code level.

There is also **RANDATA**, a database that links zip codes and cities to a variety of geographies. There are three files available through RANDATA: **Geolink**, data variables for over 128,000 places in the U.S., sorted by city, county or zip code; **Ziplink**, which has zip and county codes, plus latitude and longitude coordinates for the center of a particular zip code area; and **International**, an index to almost 93,000 locations worldwide.

The firm also publishes the annual **Commercial Atlas & Marketing Guide**, which contains state maps, statistics, and indexes, population summaries, and data on economics, transportation and communications. They have a new publication out called the **Zip Code Market Atlas & Planner**, which combines their national, regional, and local-level road atlas maps with clear film sheets containing current five-digit zip code boundaries.

MAPPING SERVICES

GEOGRAPHIC DATA TECHNOLOGY, INC.

Molly Hutchins
Manager of
Cartographic Databases
13 Dartmouth College
Hwy.
Lyme, NH 03768-9713
603-795-2183

SPECIALTY
Cartographic databases
for use with mapping
software

GDT supplies boundary and metropolitan street network files for use with mapping software on mainframe and mini-computers. One of their main products is **DYNA-MAP/USA**, a database of digitized street segments and non-street features for about 300 metropolitan areas, and the basis for an extensive line of other cartographic products and services. The firm is also well-known for its nationwide boundary files—the foundation for thematic mapping—which are especially valuable for anyone who wants to break down customer data into virtually any geographic area.

URBAN DATA PROCESSING INC.

Robert G. Coyne
President
25 Linnell Circle
Billerica, MA 01821-
3961
617-667-9955

SPECIALTY
Geocoding address
files

UDP specializes in geographic coding, or geocoding, of address records. Geocoding is the process whereby addresses are segmented by FIPS state code, county, MSA, MCD, census tract, census block group/enumeration district, zip code, or postal carrier route. By combining the geocoded addresses with information about the demographics and lifestyles of certain markets, you can thus pinpoint where your best customers live and target your promotions toward them and similar neighborhoods.

SOFTWARE FIRMS

(Also see Mapping Software and Demographic Data Companies.)

ACCOUNTLINE

Barry Raduta, Sr. V.P.,
Business Development
115 West Ave. Ste. 300
Jenkintown, PA 19046
215-572-1600

SPECIALTY
Financial marketing

Accountline has an analytic software program for financial marketers. It runs on a "Black"—or Bernoulli—Box, and integrates current estimates and five-year projections with information obtained from interviewing close to 100,000 consumers about their demographics, incomes, financial behavior, etc. The information can be further combined with data from the user's company to profile customers by a wide variety of geographies. The data are also available online.

CHADWYCK-HEALEY

Alan B. Fox, Director,
Customer Service
1101 King St.
Alexandria, VA 22314
800-752-0515

SPECIALTY
1980 census data

Chadwyck-Healey provides 1980 census and other data on a CD-ROM, and a program called **Supermap** to retrieve, manipulate and display the data in map or tabular form. The program also allows you to enter local data, and it operates on an IBM PC/XT/AT with hard disk, or compatible, 512K RAM, and a CD-ROM drive.

CONTEMPORARY TECHNOLOGY CORP.

Bernie Peterson
P.O. Box 6711
Houston, TX 77265
713-661-2555

SPECIALTY
Direct marketing

CTC develops and installs the **Geobase Update System**, customized software for demographic analysis, address matching, and election district analysis. It runs on an HP 3000 or IBM-AT and compatibles.

GSI/TACTICS

Spencer Joyner
204 Andover St.
Andover, MA 01810
617-470-3760

SPECIALTY
Sales planning

GSI/Tactics provides the **Sales Territory Planning System**, which runs on an 80286- or 80386-based workstation, and allows you to design and analyze sales territories. It can map and manipulate market data along with territory definitions at any level of geography, and produces maps, graphs, and spreadsheets; color hardcopy maps and graphs can be produced using an attached color plotter. Flexible pan and zoom functions also allow you to quickly enlarge and display any segment of a map.

STATISTICAL INNOVATIONS INC.

Jay Magidson
President
375 Concord Ave.
Belmont, MA 02178
617-489-4490

Specialty
Statistical software

Statistical Innovations is the creator of **SI-CHAID**, a segmentation software program that analyzes response to test mailings and identifies target segments; SI-CHAID operates on an IBM mainframe. The firm also develops custom software and conducts training seminars on segmentation analysis, log-linear modeling, and other advanced statistical techniques.

WALONICK ASSOCIATES

Leon Storm
Sales Manager
6500 Nicollet Ave. S.
Minneapolis, MN
55423
612-866-9022

Specialty
Statistical software

Walonick Associates provides **Stat-Packets**, modules which analyze data from Lotus 1-2-3 worksheets. They perform a variety of functions and you can purchase any combination of them; they all work with the same menu and run on IBM-PCs and compatibles with at least 256K. The marketing research Stat-Packet bundle includes Data Lister, Frequencies, Multiple Response, Crosstabs, Banners, Descriptive Statistics, and Breakdown Analysis. The firm also offers **StatPac Gold**, an independent statistics program which can handle more than 32,000 cases and up to 500 variables.

MARKET RESEARCH FIRMS

There are thousands of market research firms, but we concentrate here on those that have a demographic "angle" to their products and services.

Six Tips on How to Choose a Research Company
by Marjorie Michitti, Chilton Research Services

1. Decide whether you need a full-service research firm or a field-service firm.
A full-service firm handles an entire market research project—designing the research study; developing the sampling plan; collecting, tabulating, and analyzing the data; and presenting the results. Field service firms usually only collect data. If your project is narrowly focused, and you know who you want to talk to and what questions to ask, then a field service firm may be all you need. If your project is large, or your staffing is limited, consider a full-service company.

2. Make a list of potential firms and investigate their track records.
Ask for references. A firm's reputation can reveal a great deal about its ability to perform your research tasks. Consider each firm's capabilities in the areas that are critical to your project. These areas include survey and questionnaire design, sampling, personal interviews, telephone interviews, focus groups, mall intercepts, data analysis, and presentation. Cross off your list the firms that don't measure up.

3. Visit the firms that remain on your list.

Second-hand information is not good enough—visit each firm personally. Meet with those who will be involved in your project, including the account executive, the study director, the sampling statistician, the data collection manager and the data analyst. Talk to them about how they will handle your project.

4. Ask for proposals.

Once you've narrowed the choice down to three firms, give the companies identical specifications for your project at the same time. Ask them for creative ideas and alternative approaches to your project. Allow at least one week for the firms to respond. Don't expect a firm to give you a questionnaire in its initial proposal, but do expect an outline of the kinds of questions that the company plans to include.

5. Negotiate.

When you receive proposals, don't look just at the bottom line. If you like one company's approach but can't afford the price, ask the company how it can do your project within your budget. Don't take one company's creative design and ask other companies whether they can do it for less money. If you do this, you may have a hard time finding a firm that will invest creative time in your next project.

6. Be realistic.

Once you choose a company, ask for a timetable. Be realistic in setting your deadlines. Expect the company to deliver the results on time, but remember that haste in research can mean cutting corners on quality.

—Reprinted from American Demographics magazine.

AMERICAN SPORTS DATA, INC.

Harvey Lauer
31 Rockledge Rd.
Harsdale, NY 10530
914-472-8877

SPECIALTY
Sports and leisure
markets

Every January, American Sports Data conducts a mail panel survey in which 15,000 households are asked about such sports and leisure activities as aerobics, physical conditioning with equipment, tennis, etc. They are also questioned about favorite sports, health club membership, and how often they participate. The results are available in a summary report and in analyses of each sport or activity.

ELECTION DATA SERVICES, INC.

Kimball W. Brace
President
1522 K Street., NW
Suite 626
Washington, DC 20005
202-789-2004

SPECIALTY
Political research

EDS provides research and consultation for all levels of government, Democratic Party candidates or organizations, labor unions, trade associations, and others interested in the electoral process. Their emphasis is on developing databases for political and demographic analysis, and one of their chief products is **GeoPol**, a campaign database and targeting system that combines election, census, and political geography data. Available online, GeoPol's reports can be supported and illustrated by computer generated maps. EDS also has special programs for designing and analyzing redistricting plans.

FULTON RESEARCH GROUP

George A. Fulton
President
11351 Random Hills
Road, 4th Fl.
Fairfax, VA 22030
703-359-1720

SPECIALTY
Housing industry

The Fulton Research Group provides a variety of services for people involved in real estate development: market area analysis to help define what produce lines are most marketable and at what prices; specific site analysis, to determine the best type of house to build; planned unit development study, which analyzes long-range demand for housing; pricing studies, consumer surveys, critiques and analyses of existing projects, and, of course, consultation as to what decision should be made based on their findings.

INFORMATION RESOURCES, INC.

Forrest Anderson
150 N. Clinton St.
Chicago, IL 60606
312-726-1221

SPECIALTY
Packaged goods

IRI began with **BehaviorScan**, which uses UPC scanners to monitor the daily purchases of 3,500 households in ten cities across the U.S. These households have an electronic device attached to their TVs which controls their exposure to advertising, thus allowing clients to test ads and ad spending.

Another service from IRI is **InfoScan**, which tracks consumer purchasing for UPC-coded products sold in supermarkets across the country, together with all the promotional activities that motivate purchasing. InfoScan is further integrated with individual household purchase data, which are available through the **Marketing Fact Book service**.

IRI's other products and services include **Assessor**, which assesses new product viability; **PromotionScan**, a syndicated service which identifies winning promotions; and a range of analytical and modeling programs for the PC.

IMPACT RESOURCES

Patricia J. Mintos
Director of
Communications
779 Brooksedge Blvd.
Columbus, OH 43081
614-899-1563

SPECIALTY
Local consumer
shopping patterns

Impact Resources' data are available through MA*RT, or **Market Audience*Readership Traffic**, a database of information gathered from more than 150,000 consumers in over 17 major markets. In each market 5,000 to 10,000 consumers answer a self-administered questionnaire which asks about their demographics, shopping patterns, lifestyles, media preferences, etc. The data are available through custom and preformatted reports.

MARKET OPINION RESEARCH

John P. McDonald
Vice President
243 West Congress
Detroit, MI 48226
314-963-2414

SPECIALTY
Financial services,
utilities, health care
markets

MOR, a full-service research firm, provides a **Custom Targeting service** which identifies who your best customers are, determines where they live and produces a list so you can reach them—by mail, phone, or door-to-door—and then tracks the results. The firm, one of the top 46 U.S. research companies, also provides computer models, databases, and software programs, plus a wide variety of reports, including: Hospital Positioning Studies for Planning and Marketing, Health Screening Research Projects, Money Management and Investor Services Studies, Customer Service Studies, and Public Affairs and Communications Studies. MOR also does geodemographic analysis and other research for political campaigns.

MARKETING EVALUATIONS, INC.

Steven Levitt, President
14 Vanderventer Ave.
Port Washington, NY
11050
516-944-7775

SPECIALTY
Audiences and brand-
name consumers

If you've ever toyed with the idea of hiring the Road Runner as a company spokesman, Marketing Evaluations can give you the demographics of who responds to this character and others like him. The firm also monitors the demographics of audiences favoring specific actors, fashion designers, brand names, cartoons, movies, and TV and cable programs.

Plus, the firm has a 25,000-member national consumer household panel which is available for mail and telephone studies. The panel is balanced for six demographic variables within nine census regions, with special selections available for black and Hispanic households.

NFO RESEARCH, INC.

Melanie A. Mumper
Marketing Support
2700 Oregon Rd.,
Box 315
Toledo, OH 43691-
0315
419-666-8800

SPECIALTY
Households

NFO gathers its research through a 350,000-plus household panel, which is balanced to U.S. census data by market size, geographic division, age of householder, household income and size, and a representative mix of both family and non-family households; it is also balanced within each of nine geographic divisions. Therefore, researchers can select a sample which matches their survey requirements. NFO can conduct virtually any type of data collection for a wide variety of research studies, the results of which can be combined with the major psychographic and cluster systems.

NIELSEN MARKETING RESEARCH

(Call for a local sales
representative.)
Nielsen Plaza
Northbrook, IL 60062
312-498-6300

SPECIALTY
Food, drug, health and
beauty-aid, alcoholic-
beverage industries

Nielsen's wide range of products and services includes:
• **SCANTRACK U.S. Service**, which uses UPC scanners to provide consumer sales, pricing, and other supermarket information.
• **Nielsen Food Index**, which reports on the findings of SCANTRACK.
• **Health and Beauty Aid Service**, which covers the HBA market.

- **ERIM TESTSIGHT Service**, which provides test facilities by linking grocery and retail drugstore activity, consumer panel purchasing and TV viewing patterns.
- **Custom Audit Service**, which helps clients design and select customized marketing areas.
- **Store Observation Service**, which supplements SCAN-TRACK reports with observation checks of such things as distribution, facings, prices, displays, etc.

THE NPD GROUP

Lanny Katz, Admin.
Vice President
900 West Shore Rd.
Port Washington, NY
11050-0402
516-625-0700

SPECIALTY
Packaged and non-packaged goods;
restaurant and food-service industry

The NPD Group is divided into several divisions, including:
- **Packaged Goods**, which specializes in tracking and analyzing the purchasing and consumption patterns of basic products.
- **Special Industry Services**, which tracks information about non-packaged goods purchasing, behavior, and attitudes.
- **CREST**, which tracks and analyzes behavior trends in the restaurant and food-service industry.

PERSONNEL RESEARCH, INC.

Harold Thompson
Director of Marketing
1901 Chapel Hill Rd.
Durham, NC 27707
919-493-7534

SPECIALTY
Affirmative action
planning

PRI offers data on 514 occupational categories and 25 selected summary categories by race and gender; they are available in print, on disk, or on tape. Their software packages include **Jobpoint**, which helps users assess the relationship of job requirements to earnings; **Tracker**, for monitoring recruitment efforts; and **Data Weighter**, which weights and combines availability percentages for geographic regions and occupational categories. The firm also provides **AAPlanner II**, a microcomputer program to assist with affirmative action planning.

SAMI/BURKE

Frank Smith
Dir. of Comm.
800 Broadway
Cincinnati, OH 45202
513-852-4898

SPECIALTY
Packaged goods

A full-service research company, SAMI/Burke is divided into four divisions:
• SAMI uses UPC scanners to track retail sales, warehouse withdrawals and weekly sales of supermarket items.
• **BASES** identifies the effects of media and promotional activities on new and established brands.
• **Test Marketing** uses panel households equipped with TV meters and in-home data wands to track consumer purchase behavior and buying influences.
• Burke Marketing Research does copy testing and custom research.

SOCIOECONOMICS

Jack Lessinger
President
17004 - 26th Ave., NE
Seattle, WA 98155
206-382-9658

SPECIALTY
Real estate

Basing his strategy on the migratory patterns of Americans over the past 200 years, and considering the ways in which economic trends and social attitudes affect property values, Dr. Lessinger specializes in analyzing where the best places are to invest for long-term profit. Population data for 1982 through 1985 show that his favored counties grew at a rate that is 78.6 percent greater than the average for all U.S. counties, so it's a theory that can be put to good use for firms considering new locations, investments, and marketing strategies.

STRATEGY RESEARCH CORP.

Gary L. Berman
Vice President
100 N.W. 37th Ave.
Miami, FL 33125
305-649-5400

SPECIALTY
Hispanic market

Strategy Research is a full-service marketing firm known for its quarterly **Hispanic Omnibus**, based on personal interviews with 1500 Hispanic adults. There are also **Black** and **Anglo Omnibuses** so you can compare the data. The firm, which is active in both Hispanic and Latin American markets, can also conduct bilingual focus groups, and does research in the areas of healthcare, real estate/site location, financial services, political polls and campaign strategies, and the black market.

SURVEY SAMPLING, INC.

Donna Zimmer
One Post Road
Fairfield, CT 06430
203-254-1410

SPECIALTY
Survey research
sampling

SSI provides custom drawn samples for just about any type of household profile or business category, in any type of geography, for telephone, mail, and in-person surveys. Their random digit telephone **Super Samples** identify residential telephones, whether they're listed in directories or not; **Listed Telephone Samples** include directory-listed households; **Business and Industrial Samples** use SIC codes to categorize all businesses with telephones; **Targeted Samples** select households by income, blacks, Hispanics, and people over age 50; and **Mail and Personal Interview Samples** offer names and addresses selected by virtually any geographic area and phone number for screenings and follow-ups. The firm also provides "long" and "short" demographic profiles of survey areas. Survey Sampling offers a nationally syndicated Yellow Pages audience measurement service through its new Directory Data division, which is described under Media Data on page 199.

TEENAGE RESEARCH UNLIMITED

Peter Zollo
Vice-President
721 N. McKinley Rd.
Lake Forest, IL 60045

SPECIALTY
Teenage market

TRU conducts the **Teenage Media/Market Study**, fielded twice a year, which measures 150 categories of product purchases, readership of magazines and newspapers, radio listening, network prime-time, daytime and cable viewing, purchase power and influence, grocery shopping behavior, athletic and non-athletic activities. The firm also conducts the **Teenage Attitudinal Study**, which questions teens about such issues as parties, career, family, money, college, sex, big business, etc. Both studies are available either in a written report or online, and subscribers can have their questions included in the surveys.

TRU also conducts personal interviews, focus groups, telephone interviews, and direct mail surveys for clients.

PSYCHOGRAPHIC RESEARCH FIRMS

Psychographic, or lifestyle, research helps determine the products and the brands that people buy. For more information about this interesting branch of market segmentation, see "Psychographic Glitter and Gold" on page 59.

Four Tips for Getting the Most out of Psychographics

by Bickley Townsend, American Demographics

1. Use psychographics as one technique among many.
In particular, don't expect that you can substitute psychographics for demographics. Psychographic insights often build on demographics, and many marketers believe that psychographics are demographically driven.

2. Know how you will use psychographics.
Be sure your expectations are realistic. "Lay out your objectives for the research and make sure you're clear on what you want to get out of it," advises marketing manager Diane Hillyard of Campbell Soup. "Then predict how the study might be used. If no one knows what they'd do or how they could use the results, don't do the study!"

3. Let the buyer beware.
The old adage is applicable to anyone seeking to develop or acquire a psychographic segmentation system. Whatever the system, keep asking questions until you get satisfactory answers about how it is designed, tested, and validated. Ideally, you should validate the system yourself against your own data, including customer databases and survey information. The test is whether it works for a particular product, and whether it predicts differences in behavior among consumers.

4. Never stop monitoring the marketplace.
No matter how confident you are in a psychographic segmentation system, keep monitoring its appropriateness over time and across product categories, because values and lifestyles are constantly changing. As people move from one lifestyle to another, they shift in their attitudes, beliefs, and consumption patterns.

—Reprinted from American Demographics magazine.

LANGER ASSOCIATES, INC.

Judith Langer
President
19 W. 44th St.
New York, NY 10036
212-391-0350

Langer Associates specializes in qualitative studies of social and marketing issues. The firm's products and services include **The Langer Report**, a quarterly syndicated newsletter on changing values and lifestyles; consulting services on changing lifestyles and demographic groups; **Langer Syndicated Studies**, which are sponsored by clients and examine such markets as male homemakers and working women; focus groups; personal and telephone interviews; and brainstorming with consumers and company personnel to develop marketing and product ideas.

VALUES AND LIFESTYLES (VALS) PROGRAM

SRI International
Deborah Moroney
Director of Marketing
333 Ravenswood Ave.
Menlo Park, CA
94025-3493
415-859-2518 or 5874

The VALS Program groups adults according to their values, attitudes, needs, wants, beliefs, and demographics. They are divided into four major categories—the Need-Drivens, the Outer-Directeds, the Inner-Directeds, and the Integrated—which are further subdivided into nine lifestyle types, ranging from Survivors to Belongers to I-Am-Mes. The results are incorporated into the four cluster analysis systems.

New members of the VALS Program must buy **Orientation to VALS**, which includes reports and videotapes explaining the system, a full-day training session, limited consultation with the VALS staff, and attendance at the VALS Membership Conference. After that, users can participate in its **Leading Edge Research**, which tracks changes in the VALS typology; **Marketing Data and Services**, which provides access to their databases and research services; the **VALS Classification System**, which helps users classify their own customers; and consulting and custom research by the VALS staff.

YANKELOVICH CLANCY SHULMAN

Cindy Payea
8 Wright Street
Westport, CT 06880
203-227-2700 or
212-752-7500

Yankelovich Clancy Shulman is known for **The Monitor**, a 16-year-old service which interviews 2,500 respondents around the country in order to gauge consumer social values and attitudes. It currently tracks 55 trends and segments the respondents into six groups: the New Autonomous, Gamesmen, Scramblers, Traditionals, American Dreamers, and the Aimless. Along the same lines is **Senior Monitor**, which studies the values and attitudes of people over 50.

Other services include **Perceptual Scan**, which tracks customers' attitudes toward your products; **Data Recast**, with which the firm analyzes customer data; and **Litmus Optimization**, a mathematical model which can help define and solve a variety of marketing problems.

OPINION POLLING FIRMS

As anyone who has ever followed a political campaign knows, determining what Americans think—which frequently is not what they do—is of the utmost importance to shaping strategy. The following firms provide a variety of services which help business, politicians, and others understand the needs and wants of their target audiences.

CAMBRIDGE REPORTS, INC.

David E. Williams
Senior Vice President
675 Massachusetts Ave.
Cambridge, MA 02139
617-661-0110

Cambridge Reports conducts quarterly national consumer and public opinion surveys and an annual national opinion leader survey on a variety of issues ranging from business and labor, to healthcare, to lifestyles. The results are published in a series of reports, and the data are also available online through three databases. Clients can have their questions included in the national omnibus surveys. The firm also provides consulting services.

THE GALLUP ORGANIZATION, INC.

Andrew Kohut
President
53 Bank St., Box 310
Princeton, NJ 08542
609-924-9600

Gallup conducts the bi-weekly personal interview **Gallup Omnibus,** along with regular telephone omnibus surveys, multi-sponsored surveys of consumer behavior and attitudes, and local market surveys.

OPINION RESEARCH SERVICE

Dennis Gilbert
President
P.O. Box 9076,
J.F.K. Station
Boston, MA 02114
617-840-1178

Opinion Research publishes the annual **American Public Opinion Index,** in which the questions asked in other firms' surveys are listed alphabetically by topic. The responses are available on microfiche in **American Public Opinion Data,** which also includes the exact wording of the questions and the polling methodology. Topics covered include business and economics, communications and journalism, crime and corrections, education, government and public policy, health, religion, etc.

THE ROPER ORGANIZATION, INC.

Richard Baxter
Senior Vice President
205 E. 42nd St.
New York, NY 10017
212-599-0700

The Roper Organization is known for its continuous market/opinion research service which measures consumer behavior and public attitudes toward major business, social, and political issues. Every five weeks, 2,000 Americans, divided into 40 demographic subgroups, are interviewed in their homes, and firms can have their questions included in the survey through **Limobus**. The results are available online—allowing subscribers to run custom tabulations—or through ten annual **Roper Reports**.

AUDIENCE MEASUREMENT FIRMS

From magazines to radio stations to cable television, all media that accept advertising are anxious to prove that they've got the best "numbers"—that is, proof that their audience is larger and more desirable than the people tuning into their competition. Using a variety of technological and statistical measures, the following firms help media demonstrate the size and demographic quality of their readers, listeners, and viewers.

AGB TELEVISION RESEARCH

Bob Hoffman
540 Madison Ave.
New York, NY 10022
212-319-8800

SPECIALTY
Estimating television
audiences

AGB is famous—or, in some circles, infamous—for its **PeopleMeter,** which monitors what television programs are being watched by each member of the several thousand households designated in its sample. Every person in the sample is assigned a number which he or she presses into the PeopleMeter handset whenever they start or stop watching TV. Every 24 hours the data are gathered through a collector box in each household. AGB also monitors VCR audiences, and can provide detailed information about the demographics, cable status, etc., of the members of its sample.

ARBITRON RATINGS COMPANY

Katie Bachman
1350 Avenue of
the Americas
New York, NY 10019
212-887-1300

SPECIALTY
Estimating media
audiences

Arbitron measures audiences in 213 television and 259 radio markets. They provide their estimates for specific television programs and for any radio or television daypart. Audiences can be described by such geographic areas as zip code, county, ADI, or metro market, and they can be further segmented into various demographic, socioeconomic, lifestyle, and purchasing pattern groups. A relatively new division of Arbitron is **ScanAmerica**, a syndicated research service that uses a people meter to electronically track television viewing of each individual and a portable UPC scanner to record product purchases by the household.

DIRECTORY DATA

Matt Cone
Account Executive
One Post Road
Fairfield, CT 06430
203-255-4200

SPECIALTY
Estimating Yellow
Pages audiences

Directory Data, a division of Survey Sampling, a firm long known for survey research sampling (see its listing under Market Research firms, page 193), offers a nationally syndicated Yellow Pages audience measurement service, which provides annual audience estimates for individual markets and directory coverage areas. Subscribers receive reports at the end of each 12-month data collection cycle. A new service, the first reports will be available by the end of 1988.

MEDIAMARK RESEARCH INC.

Sylvia Cassel
Senior Vice President,
Administration
341 Madison Ave.
New York, NY 10017
212-599-0444

SPECIALTY
Estimating media
audiences

Each year MRI surveys the demographics and media and product usage of 20,000 adults in 48 states. The data, which are available online and in written reports, detail how many people are watching network and cable television, listening to the radio, reading magazines and newspapers, and buying a wide range of products. MRI also combines its media and product usage data with the four cluster systems.

MENDELSOHN MEDIA RESEARCH, INC.

Jacqueline Toback
Sr. Vice President,
Director of Marketing
352 Park Ave. South
New York, NY 10010
212-684-6350

SPECIALTY
The affluent market

Mendelsohn's 1987 **Survey of Adults and Markets of Affluence** is their eleventh study of adults in 48 states who have household incomes of $50,000 or more. In it they report on what publications, television programs, radio format, and radio networks attract the affluent, and supplement their findings with data from the Census Bureau's 1986 and 1987 Current Population Surveys. There is also information on such topics as public activities, airline travel, hotel/motel stays, VCR and athletic equipment expenditures, etc. The complete survey is available in a six-volume report and on computer tape.

NATIONAL YELLOW PAGES SERVICES ASSOCIATION

Karen Jones
888 W. Big Beaver Rd.
Troy, NY 48084
313-362-7890

SPECIALTY
Estimating Yellow
Pages audiences

Among its services and reports, NYPSA offers a demographic analysis package called TYM, or **Target Your Market**, which provides four sets of data: Demographics, Business Statistics, ClusterPlus (a cluster analysis system from Donnelley Marketing), and Directory Cost Analysis. Useful for deciding where to place Yellow Pages directory advertising, TYM is available in both standardized and custom reports.

NIELSEN MEDIA RESEARCH

(Call for a local sales
representative.)
Nielsen Plaza
Northbrook, IL 60062-
6288
312-498-6300

Specialty
Estimating television
audiences

Nielsen estimates broadcast and cable television audiences through the Nielsen **Television Index**, which provides national network ratings by using electronic meters—or People Meters—in a sample of households across the country. Nielsen **Station Index** supplies viewing reports for each of 220 local television markets at least four times a year, reports which are analyzed to reveal how many families—and what numbers and type of people—use their TV sets at any given moment.

R.D. PERCY & COMPANY

Rick Spicer, Senior
Vice President-Sales
230 Park Ave., Ste. 207
New York, NY 10169
212-972-4850

SPECIALTY
Estimating television
audiences

The Percy System measures TV commercial and program audiences with a push-button meter. The data come out in three reports: Percy **Commercial Monitor**, a monthly report which provides ratings for all network and spot commercials as well as placement details; Percy **Audience Report**, a standard monthly program audience report; and Percy **Audience Report Extended**, which is like the Audience Report, but includes more demographic breakouts. The data are also available online.

SIMMONS MARKET RESEARCH BUREAU

Kay Wall, President
Syndicated Studies Div.
219 E. 42nd St.
New York, NY 10017
212-867-1414

SPECIALTY
Estimating media
audiences

SMRB is known for its annual study of media—magazines, newspapers, television, radio, cable, outdoor, and Yellow Pages—and markets. The study combines data on media audiences, product/brand usage (almost 5,000 brands are reported on), demographics, and psychographics. The data from the study are also available on-line and through their micro system, **CHOICES**. The firm conducts other studies on the college market, local newspapers, the affluent, and teenagers, and researchers can have their questions included in the Simmons sample.

DIRECT MARKETING SERVICES

The following firms offer many lists and related services, but we only discuss those products and services that involve demographics. When buying demographically-enhanced lists, that is, lists that are broken out according to such demographic characteristics as age, income, homeownership, etc., it is important to ask how the list was compiled and how often it is updated.

GENERATION MARKETING, INC.

Jackie Geber
Account Executive
1 Lincoln Plaza
New York, NY 10023-
7177
212-496-9280

Generation Marketing has a database called **Agebase**, which contains the names and addresses of over 176 million adults and children, broken out by age and income. Each name is matched to the addressee's exact date of birth, and the entire file has been enhanced with such indicators as dwelling type, ethnicity, income, and a cluster analysis system which allows direct marketers to target lifestyles as well as demographics.

J.L. SULLIVAN, INC.

Kate A. Hallock
Senior Vice President,
General Sales Manager
101 West Mall Plaza,
Suite 103
Pittsburgh, PA 15106
412-429-8080

J.L. Sullivan has a database called **Power Play** that adds geodemographic profiles, psychographic analyses and other market-specific information to your application and accounting files. You can access it online or send your list file to J.L. Sullivan, which takes 4 to 6 weeks to process it. They then advise you on what business decisions to make based on the results.

JAMI MARKETING SERVICES, INC.

John Greany
Accounts Manager
2 Executive Dr.
Fort Lee, NJ 07024
201-461-8868

You can more accurately target prospects with JAMI's lists, which are demographically-enhanced by Donnelley Marketing (see their listing on page 170). Lists are available for everything from homeowners to *Country Music* subscribers to astrological mail order buyers—all available by age, income, sex, number of children, marital status, birth date, employment status, etc.

MCRB (Market Compilation & Research Bureau, Inc.)

(Call for a local sales
representative.)
60 E. 42nd St., Ste. 721
New York, NY 10165
212-661-1250

A full-service direct marketing firm (i.e., one that offers everything from mailing lists to merge-purge services to list management), MCRB provides lists, with selections within each, of high school students (selections include year in school, not expected to enter college, parents of, etc.), college students (year, type of college, major, etc.), families (age of children and parents), new and expectant mothers, and mature adults.

METRODIRECT

Liz Hertel
Account Executive
901 W. Bond St.
Lincoln, NE 68521-
3694
800-228-4571

MetroDirect, a division of Metromail, can identify and characterize nearly 78,000,000 households and provide you with their addresses and telephone numbers. You can specify dwelling unit size, length of residence, age, ethnic or religious surname, age and school of children, income, response to direct mail selections (e.g., people who have responded to political direct mail campaigns), and just about any other demographic characteristic.

NATIONAL DEMOGRAPHICS & LIFESTYLES

Tom Ratkovich
Dir., Information Svcs.
1621 Eighteenth Street
Denver, CO 80202-
1211
303-292-5000

National Demographics' 30-million name mailing list is based on 1 million questionnaires which are sent out every month. The questionnaire, which is self-administered, queries consumers about their demographics and lifestyles. By combining the results with geographic information, the firm provides lists that can help direct marketers more precisely target their mailings.

R.L. POLK & COMPANY

Jerry Helmicki
Manager, List Services
6400 Monroe Blvd.
Taylor, MI 48180-1814

SPECIALTY
Demographically-en-
hanced mailing lists

R.L. Polk's enormous list, futuristically named **List X-1**, is compiled through vehicle registrations, telephone lists, birth and school information, questionnaires, and other means. It is composed of the names and addresses of consumers broken out according to sex, income, home ownership, occupation, presence of children, and other demographic variables which, when further segmented by geography, can practically guarantee red-hot prospects for direct mailers' products and services.

The firm also provides **Geoplus**, a software system which assigns census tract codes to zip codes, so the addresses can then be further enhanced by cluster analysis. Geoplus operates on a mainframe computer.

Finally, there is **Household Mail Response Analysis**, which applies demographic factors to your list and then compares the results to its X-1 list, thus allowing you to determine and rank the responsiveness of the households in your file.

SMARTNAMES INC.

James F. Cunningham
Vice President, Sales
245 Winter St.
Waltham, MA 02154
617-890-5705

SmartNames has two interesting lists available: **Homes**, which is enhanced according to home type, age, size, and construction, and the demographics of the homeowners; and **Consumer**, which is broken down by consumers' age, income, sex, dwelling type, education, and specific product and service interest indicators, such as bankcards, magazines, mutual funds, life insurance, etc. There are a wide variety of geographic segmentations available for both lists. SmartNames also provides research services, profiling and analysis, modeling, and custom database development.

TRW TARGET MARKETING SERVICES

Warren Fenske
901 N. International Pkwy.
Richardson, TX 75081
800-527-3933
in Texas 800-442-4967

TRW has two databases containing over 138 million names, and from them they generate mailing lists enhanced by age, sex, income, and credit card usage. Some of their lists include prospects for fund raising, healthcare, and insurance, along with lists of new movers, families with children, and Hispanics. The firm also provides **Risk and Response Models**, which incorporate credit and demographic information, and other services to target your mailings.

CONSULTANTS

ECONOMIC RESEARCH SERVICES, INC.

Leonard T. Elzie
4901 Tower Court,
Suite 200
Tallahassee, FL 32303
904-562-1211

SPECIALTY
Equal employment op-
portunity

The economists at ERS develop computerized databases to monitor corporate employment and compensation practices, develop and update affirmative action plans, and serve as expert witnesses in the areas of statistical analysis, labor economics, employment discrimination, and wage forecasts.

OSTROFF ASSOCIATES

Jeffrey M. Ostroff
President
114 Chatham Place
Wilmington, DE 19810
302-475-7114

SPECIALTY
The mature market

Ostroff Associates helps businesses increase their share of the 50+ market. To that end, they provide marketing research, seminars and in-house training, packaging of promotional pieces, and consulting.

SALES EVALUATION ASSOCIATES, INC.

David Glazer, President
171 Madison Ave.
New York, NY 10016
212-213-0180

SPECIALTY
Yellow Pages media
planning

In addition to being a consultant to the Yellow Pages industry, Sales Evaluation Associates applies demographic and business data to measure clients' sales potential and performance. The firm helps consumer goods and services clients, business-to-business marketers, and trade associations build and use demographic databases, analyze sales, and allocate ad budgets.

APPENDIX

THE UNITED STATES: JUST THE FACTS

by Daphne Spain, updated by Janet McClafferty

Here is a quick statistical portrait of what the population of the United States looked like in 1986.

Even in a country like the United States where demographers have the advantages of an excellent vital statistics system, frequent household surveys, and an extended history of census taking, there are still surprises that show up every ten years.

After the 1980 census, demographer Calvin Beale mentioned the following as the most important surprises of the decade:
• Birth and death rates and household size that declined more rapidly than expected.
• Migration to the Sunbelt that surpassed expectations.
• Triple the projected rate of growth in nonmetropolitan areas.
• The unanticipated significance of illegal and refugee immigration.

The following report summarizes the most recent data available for the United States.

POPULATION GROWTH AND DISTRIBUTION

On July 1, 1986, the total population of the U.S., including Armed Forces overseas, was estimated at 241.6 million, an increase of 1 percent over the 239 million estimated on July 1, 1985. (The population recorded by the census on April 1, 1980, was 226.5 million.) The birth rate in 1986 was 16 births per 1,000 persons and the death rate was

8.7 per 1,000 persons. Legal net civilian immigration was 2.6 per 1,000 population, down slightly from 2.9 in 1980, when a large number of refugees was admitted.

Ninety-one percent of national population growth between April 1, 1980 and July 1, 1986 occurred in the South and West. Alaska, Arizona, Nevada, Florida, Texas, California, and Utah had the highest rates of growth; Texas, California, and Florida together accounted for over half of total population growth.

RURAL RENAISSANCE

Although the rate of Sunbelt growth exceeded expectations during the 1970s, its growth was less surprising than the "rural renaissance." Between 1970 and 1980, the rural population grew from 54 million to 60 million, the largest numerical gain since the 1870s. The 11.1 percent increase in rural areas was the highest rate of growth since the 1890s, almost equalling the urban growth rate of 11.6 percent. This turnaround was due to growth in the rural nonfarm population, since the farm population accounted for 2.2 percent of the total population in 1986.

Rural and urban areas are defined by population density and are not the same as nonmetropolitan and metropolitan areas—which are defined as whole counties (towns and cities in New England) linked socially and economically to an urban core.

There can be rural people in metropolitan areas and urban people in nonmetropolitan areas. The nonmetropolitan population of 57 million in 1980 consisted of 35 million rural people and 22 million urban people. Metropolitan areas contained approximately 75 percent of the population in 1980. During the 1970s, metropolitan areas grew by 10 percent compared with 15 percent for nonmetropolitan areas and 11 percent for the country as a whole. This was a reversal from the previous decade, when MSAs grew 17 percent and nonmetropolitan areas grew only 3 percent.

Some nonmetropolitan growth is due to development on the fringes of metropolitan areas. But much is due to growth in remote counties where new employment opportunities have been created. Partially because of growth in employment, many of these nonmetropolitan areas grew because local residents chose to stay in the community as job opportunities opened up there rather than look for work elsewhere. These places grew less from in-migration as from a stemming of outmigration. There are limits to nonmetropolitan growth, however. One of the "Catch-22's" is that it cannot continue indefinitely, since, as nonmetropolitan areas expand, they are likely to be included in existing metropolitan areas or become reclassified as new metropolitan areas.

AGE, RACE, AND ETHNICITY

The median age of the population was exactly 30 on April 1, 1980, and was 31.8 on July 1, 1982. This means that about one-half of the population was under age 32 and one-half was over age 32. Low fertility and the aging baby-boom generation account for the rise in median age from 27.9 years in 1970.

The population aged 25 to 34 (prime household formation years) grew rapidly between 1970 and 1980, up 48 percent versus 11 percent for the total population. The elderly were also a rapidly growing group during the decade. The population aged 65 and over grew 13.5 percent, to 29 million, between 1980 and 1986. Twelve percent of the total U.S. population is elderly—the highest proportion in the nation's history. At the same time the proportion of people 65 and over is at its peak, the proportion of the population under age 15 is at its lowest level. From 1970 to 1986, this group declined from 28 to 23 percent of the total population. In 1986, there were 52 million persons under the age of 15, down from 58 million in 1970.

Minority groups grew more rapidly than the total population during the 1970s, and increased as a percentage of the total population. Between 1970 and 1980, the black population increased from 23 million to about 27 million—17 percent growth. Blacks were 12 percent of the population in 1980 compared with 11 percent in 1970. The Spanish-origin population increased from 9 million to about 15 million, a growth rate of 61 percent. Hispanics were 6 percent of the population in 1980 compared with 4.5 percent in 1970. American Indians, Eskimos, Aleuts, Asian and Pacific Islanders, and "others" equalled 5 percent of the population in 1980. Whites had the lowest rate of increase for the decade, growing only 6 percent, or from 178 to 188 million.

Today, 205 million whites compose 85 percent of the total U.S. population. Although blacks grew 7 percent between 1980 and 1986, to 29 million, they did not increase their share of the total population. The 8 million persons in the "other" category, including Native Americans and Asians, reduced their share to 3 percent.

The Hispanic population grew between 1980 and 1986, but not as much as it had in the previous decade. However, growth was still much greater than for the U.S. population as a whole: a 25 percent growth for the Hispanic population, compared to a 6 percent growth for the total U.S. population. Persons of Hispanic origin now make up 8 percent of our total population.

DIFFICULT TRENDS TO ANALYZE

Trends in population growth by race and ethnicity are difficult to analyze because of changes in the census questionnaire and in allocation procedures, and in the way people answer the race and Spanish-origin questions. For example, 93 percent of persons of Spanish origin reported themselves as white in 1970, but only 56 percent identified themselves as white in 1980. Changes in self-identification have therefore contributed to the growth of the Hispanic population as well as natural increase and both legal and illegal immigration. Some estimates are that if 1970 and 1980 procedures could be standardized, the Hispanic population would have shown a smaller increase and whites would have shown an increase of perhaps 10 percent. Minority groups have younger age structures than whites. In 1980, the median age for blacks was 25 and for Hispanics 23, compared with 31 for whites. Because of higher fertility and the tendency of younger persons of Spanish origin to immigrate to the U.S., minorities also have higher proportions of people under age 15 and lower proportions of people aged 65 and over.

There are regional differences in the distribution of minority groups. Fifty-three percent of blacks live in the South compared to 33 percent of the total population. California and Texas accounted for 52 percent of Hispanics versus only 17 percent of the total population. Higher proportions of minorities than whites live in the central cities of metropolitan areas: 58 percent of blacks, 50 percent of Hispanics, and only 25 percent of whites.

HOUSEHOLDS AND FAMILIES

The U.S. Census Bureau estimates that there were 88.5 million households in 1986, up from 63 million in 1970 and 81 million in 1980. Seventy-two percent of these were family households and 28 percent were nonfamily households. A family household is one maintained by a person living with relatives, whereas a nonfamily household includes either a person living alone or with others to whom he or she is not related. Nonfamily households grew more rapidly than family households: 109 percent versus 24 percent between 1970 and 1986. Much of the increase in nonfamily households is due to the rapid rise in the number of single-person households: from 11 million in 1970 to 21 million in 1986, or an increase of 95 percent. Married-couple households, in contrast, grew by only 14 percent during the same period (from 45 million to 51 million). Married-couple households now represent 58 percent of all households compared with 71 percent in 1970. Single-person households accounted for 24 percent of households in 1986, compared to 17 percent in 1970. The number of families headed by a woman increased from 5.5 million in 1970 to over 10 million in 1986, a rise of 86 percent. Families with female householders comprised 12 percent of all households in 1986.

Average household size declined from 3.14 persons in 1970 to 2.67 in 1986. Average family size declined from 3.60 persons to 3.21 during the same period. The smaller household size is due primarily to the increase in the number of one-person households (both among the young and the elderly) and lower fertility, which reduces the average number of children per family. The average number of children a woman will have in her lifetime was 1.8 in 1986, down about 25 percent from the 1970 rate of 2.5. The 1986 rate implies a level of fertility below that necessary for natural replacement of the population. The population will continue to grow into the 21st century, however, because of the large proportion of women currently of childbearing age.

HOUSING

The total number of housing units increased from 69 million in 1970 to 88 million in 1980, up by 29 percent. Women-occupancy rose slightly from 63 to 64 percent of all occupied units. The majority of American homes are single-family dwellings—62 percent in 1980. Row houses and townhouses accounted for only 4 percent of the nation's housing stock, while buildings of 2 to 4 units represented 11 percent of all units, and apartment complexes of 5 or more units were 18 percent of the housing stock. Five percent of all housing units were mobile homes.

Just over 50 percent of U.S. households heated with natural gas in 1980, and another 18 percent heated with fuel oil, down from 26 percent in 1970, while the proportion heating with electricity rose from 8 to 18 percent. Wood as the primary heating fuel increased from 1 percent of all households in 1970 to 3 percent in 1980. Median monthly housing costs for owners averaged $365 and for renters $243 in 1980.

EDUCATION

Approximately 58 million persons aged 3 to 34 were enrolled in public and private schools in 1983. Nursery school enrollment more than doubled from 1 to 2.4 million between 1970 and 1983, while kindergarten enrollment remained stable. Elementary school enrollment dropped from 34 to 27 million, reflecting the baby bust that followed the baby boom. High school enrollment declined slightly to 14 million. College enrollment has shown a large increase, from 7 to 11 million, partly as a result of large increases in women going to college part-time, particularly those over age 30.

The proportion of the population with a high school diploma increased significantly between 1970 and 1985. Among persons aged 25 and over, 74 percent were high school graduates in 1985 compared with 55 percent in 1970. The proportion of the population completing four or more years of college also rose, from 11 to 19 percent. These increases are due to the replacement of older people who have less education by younger, more educated people.

Men and women have approximately equal high school graduation rates. More women than men are currently enrolled in college, but more men than women have actually completed college: 23 percent of men compared with 16 percent of women in 1985. Whites are better educated than blacks. In 1985, 76 percent of whites versus 60 percent of blacks had completed high school; 20 percent of whites but only 11 percent of blacks had completed four or more years of college. Hispanics had lower levels of high school completion than blacks (48 percent), as well as a lower college completion level (9 percent).

LABOR FORCE

The civilian labor force grew from 83 million in 1970 to 118 million in 1986, rising 42 percent. Women accounted for nearly two-thirds of this growth. Since 1970, the number of women in the labor force has increased by 21 million, while the number of men increased by 14 million. In 1986, there were 52 million women and 65 million men in the labor force. Women have increased as a proportion of the total labor force, from 38 percent in 1970 to 45 percent in 1986.

The labor force participation rate refers to those employed, looking for work, or temporarily laid off from a job. The labor force participation rate for women rose from 43 percent in 1970 to 55 percent in 1986. The largest increase occurred among married women with pre-school children, a group which traditionally stays at home. Labor force participation rates for women in this category rose from 30 percent in 1970 to 51 percent in 1986.

In contrast to rising rates of labor force participation for women, men's rates have dropped slightly, from 80 to 76 percent. This is partly because of earlier retirements. The rise in female labor force participation has offset the decline in male participation, so that the overall labor force participation rate rose from 60 to 65 percent of the total population aged 16 and over between 1970 and 1986.

White-collar employment experienced the greatest growth during the 1970s and early 1980s. Professional and technical workers had the largest numerical increase, rising from 12 million in 1972 to 17 million in 1986, followed by clerical workers, who increased from 14 million to 18 million. Managerial occupations had the largest percentage increase, growing more than 40 percent between 1972 and 1986, while blue-collar employment grew from 29 million workers to 34 million. In 1986, 40 percent of all unemployed workers were in blue-collar occupations.

Although men are fairly evenly distributed among all occupations, almost four-fifths of women were concentrated in four major occupation groups: clerical workers, 29 percent; service workers, 18 percent; professional workers, 18 percent, mostly in nursing and teaching; and operatives, except transport, 8 percent.

INCOME AND POVERTY

Median family income in 1985 was $23,600, a figure virtually unchanged from that in 1975 in constant dollars. Part of the slow growth in real family income is attributed to the increase in the proportion of families with a female householder, a group with a lower median income than any other type of family ($13,500 in 1985).

White families had a median income of $24,900 in 1985, not significantly different from their 1975 level in real terms. Black family median income in 1985, $14,800, was lower than that of whites, but also was not significantly lower than their 1975 income. Fifty-six percent of families had two or more wage earners in 1985. About 15 percent had no earners; e.g., the retired or those receiving welfare benefits, and 29 percent had one earner only.

Recently there has been a rise in the proportion of the population below the poverty level, which was defined as $11,000 for a family of four in 1985. About 14 percent of the population was below the poverty level in 1985, compared with 12 percent in both 1979 and 1969. The number of persons classified as poor increased from 26 million in 1979 to 33 million in 1985.

Although there were more poor people in 1985 than in 1969, the incidence of poverty among the elderly has declined from 25 percent of those aged 65 and over, to 13 percent. This decline is partly due to indexing of Social Security benefits to keep pace with inflation. There are significant differences in poverty status by race: The poverty rate for whites in 1985 was 11 percent, considerably lower than the black rate (31 percent) and the Hispanic rate (29 percent).

PROJECTIONS FOR THE FUTURE

The failure of earlier projections to accurately predict all the changes that occurred in the 1970s does not deter demographers from offering projections for the 1990s. Most of the trends of the 1970s are expected to continue, with low fertility rates prevailing. The number of households is expected to increase, while the average household size declines even further, possibly to 2.5 by 1990. The population shift to the Sunbelt will continue, but not as rapidly as in the 1970s. Nonmetropolitan growth may slacken if employment opportunities decline in a lagging economy. The total U.S. population is projected to be 250 million by 1990, 260 million in 1995, and 268 million by the year 2000.

USEFUL
PUBLICATIONS

...from the Federal Government

User's Guide to the Bureau of Economic Analysis
BEA, U.S. Department of Commerce, 1401 K St., NW, Washington, DC 20230; free.

Census Catalog and Guide
Superintendent of Documents, Government Printing Office, Washington, DC 20402; 202-783-3238; about $21.

Survey of Income and Program Participation Users' Guide
Customer Services, Bureau of the Census, Washington, DC 20233; 301-763-4100; $10.

How to Gain Access to Bureau of Justice Statistics Data
Superintendent of Documents, Government Printing Office, Washington, DC 20402; free.

Telephone Contacts at the Bureau of Justice Statistics
Superintendent of Documents, Government Printing Office, Washington, DC 20402; free.

Major Programs of the Bureau of Labor Statistics
Office of Inquiries and Correspondence, U.S. Bureau of Labor Statistics, 441 G St., NW, Rm. 2831A, Washington, DC 20212; 202-523-1221 or 1222; free.

Bureau of Labor Statistics Update
(lists new BLS publications)
Office of Inquiries and Correspondence, U.S. Bureau of Labor Statistics, 441 G St., NW, Rm. 2831A, Washington, DC 20212; 202-523-1221 or 1222; free.

Bureau of Labor Statistics
Data Files on Tape
Bureau of Labor Statistics, Division of Special Publications, Washington, DC 20212; 202-523-1090; free.

Economic Research Service Reports
(lists new ERS publications)
Information Division, Economic Research Service, 1301 New York Ave., NW, Washington, DC 20250; free.

Catalog of Publications from the Center for Education Statistics
Education Information Office, Center for Education Statistics, Department of Education, Washington, DC 20208; 800-424-1616; 800-626-9854 in Washington, DC; free.

National Center for
Health Statistics Catalogs
Scientific and Technical Information Branch, National Center for Health Statistics, U.S. Dept. of Health and Human Services, 3700 East-West Hwy., Rm. 157, Hyattsville, MD 20782; 301-436-8500; free.

National Technical Information
Service General Catalog
NTIS, 5285 Port Royal Rd., Springfield, VA 22161; free.

Social Security Administration
Research and Statistics
Publications Catalog
Office of Research and Statistics, Social Security Administration, U.S. Dept. of Health and Human Services, 4301 Connecticut Ave., NW, Washington, DC 20008; free.

Office of Information Management
and Statistics Publications
(describes reports available from the Veterans Administration)
Office of Information Management and Statistics, Statistical Policy and Research Service, Veterans Administration, 810 Vermont Ave., NW, Washington, DC 20420; 202-233-2563; free.

USEFUL PUBLICATIONS
...from American Demographics

The following items can all be ordered directly from American Demographics, P.O. Box 68, Ithaca, NY 14851. Either send in your order with payment, or call American Demographics' toll free line, 800-828-1133, and charge to your MasterCard, Visa, or American Express account.

Marketing Tools Alert
A catalog of books, audiocassettes, and other products of use to marketers. Free.

American Demographics Magazine
Examines consumer trends, lifestyles, buying behavior, and media preferences. Monthly, $48/year.

The Numbers News
A newsletter of key marketing information, up-to-the-minute data, and concise analysis of consumer trends. Monthly, $149/year.

100 Predictions for the Baby Boom
by Cheryl Russell
A book about every aspect of the baby boom: their families, work, money, and much more. 249 pages; $17.95, plus $2 for shipping.

The Dictionary of Demography
by Roland Pressat,
edited by Christopher Wilson
A user-friendly demographic sourcebook for non-demographers. 243 pages; $60.00, plus $2 for shipping.

The Population of the U.S.: Historical Trends and Future Projections
by Donald Bogue
An in-depth look at population growth, composition, social, economic, political, religious, and housing characteristics. A big event in demographic publishing. 728 pages; $100.00, plus $2 for shipping.

Guide to Statistical Materials Produced by Governments and Associations in the U.S.
by Stratford & Stratford
A useful directory of publications that are available to the public and that cost under $100. 279 pages; $85.00, plus $2 for shipping.

CONTRIBUTORS

Below is the list of the experts who participated in *The Insider's Guide to Demographic Know-How*. Their pieces originally appeared in American Demographics magazine.

Michael Batutis is technical director of CACI in Fairfax, Virginia.

Marci Belcher was formerly marketing manager for MPSI Systems, Inc., in San Francisco.

John Chapman is director of research for the International Council of Shopping Centers, New York.

Diane Crispell is associate editor of The Numbers News, research associate of American Demographics, and an associate editor of American Demographics magazine.

Thomas Exter is research director of American Demographics, and a senior editor of American Demographics magazine.

Peter Francese is president and founder of American Demographics.

Janet McClafferty is research assistant of American Demographics.

Marjorie Michitti is vice president and group manager at Chilton Research Services, Radnor, Pennsylvania.

Dowell Myers is assistant professor of real estate and urban land economics, School of Business at the University of Wisconsin–Madison.

Marvin Nesbit is director of the Small Business Development Center at Florida International University, Miami, Florida, and is the president and general manager of Pro-Mark Services, a marketing consulting firm.

William O'Hare is director of policy studies, Population Reference Bureau, Washington, DC, and a contributing editor of American Demographics magazine.

James Paris is a senior associate at Urban Decision Systems, Inc. All estimates in his piece, "How to Read a Demographic Report," are by Urban Decision Systems.

Daphne Spain is a freelance writer and a former contributing editor to American Demographics magazine.

Bickley Townsend is director of research and education, American Demographics, and a senior editor of American Demographics magazine.

Arthur Weinstein is regional manager/marketing analyst for the Small Business Development Center at Florida State University, Miami, Florida.

GLOSSARY

A

ADI Area of Dominant Influence, a television market, as defined by Arbitron, a firm which measures TV audiences. (See *television market*.)

audience measurement methods Methods to determine who is listening to radio and watching TV.

B

baby boom The large generation of Americans born between 1946 and 1964.

baby boomlet (echo boom) Children of the baby boom, born between 1977 and the present.

baby bust The generation born between 1965 and 1976, when birth rates dropped rapidly and remained low.

benchmark An area against which you compare an area you're studying. Some good benchmarks are reports on the United States as a whole, and reports for the state, metropolitan area, county, or city in which a site is located.

birth rate Number of births a year per 1000 population.
 • **general fertility rate** Number of births a year per 1000 women aged 15 to 44.
 • **total fertility rate** Number of live births per 1000 women in their lifetime; an approximation of completed family size.

blocks Census administrative areas, generally equivalent to city blocks.

block groups Groups of blocks, averaging 1,000 to 1,200 population; the major advantage of using block groups over blocks in area analysis is that more data are available for block groups.

boundary The border around a market area that is being studied.

boundary files Geography—streets, railroads, blocks, and census tracts—that is described in a manner that is understandable to a computer.

C

CENSPAC A computer program developed by the Census Bureau to manipulate its computer files from the 1980 census.

census The official collection of information on the demographic, social, and economic situation of all people residing in a specified area at a certain time.
• **divisions** The nine census divisions are:
   1. Pacific: Alaska, California, Hawaii, Oregon, Washington
   2. Mountain: Arizona, Colorado, Idaho, Montana, Nevada, New Mexico, Utah, Wyoming,
   3. West North Central: Iowa, Kansas, Minnesota, Missouri, Nebraska, North Dakota, South Dakota
   4. East North Central: Illinois, Indiana, Michigan, Ohio, Wisconsin
   5. West South Central: Arkansas, Louisiana, Oklahoma, Texas
   6. East South Central: Alabama, Kentucky, Mississippi, Tennessee
   7. South Atlantic: West Virginia, Delaware, Florida, Georgia, Maryland, North Carolina, South Carolina, Virginia, Washington, DC
   8. Middle Atlantic: New Jersey, New York, Pennsylvania, Rhode Island
   9. New England: Connecticut, Maine, Massachusetts, New Hampshire, Vermont
• **geography** The U.S. Census Bureau collects and publishes data for many government and statistical areas
• **government areas** U.S., Puerto Rico, and outlying areas under U.S. sovereignty or jurisdiction; states, counties, and county equivalents; incorporated places and minor civil divisions; Congressional districts and election precincts; American Indian reservations and Alaska Native villages
• **statistical areas** Four census regions and nine census divisions, all of which are groupings of states; metropolitan areas; census county divisions in states where minor

civil division boundaries are not satisfactory for statistical purposes; census designated places; urbanized areas; census tracts and subdivisions of counties averaging about 4,000 people; census blocks; enumeration districts; block groups.

• **maps** The Census Bureau publishes two kinds of maps:
>   1. Outline maps that show the names and boundaries of the geographic areas for which data are produced
>   2. Statistical maps that display selected data by the use of color and shading.

• **products** Information from the census is available in printed reports, microfiche, computer tape, online, in diskettes, and on maps.

• **regions** The four census regions are
>   1. West: Washington, Oregon, California, Idaho, Montana, Wyoming, Colorado, New Mexico, Arizona, Utah, and Nevada
>   2. Midwest: North Dakota, South Dakota, Nebraska, Kansas, Missouri, Iowa, Minnesota, Wisconsin, Illinois, Indiana, Ohio, and Michigan
>   3. South: Texas, Oklahoma, Arkansas, Louisiana, Mississippi, Alabama, Florida, Georgia, South Carolina, North Carolina, Virginia, Washington, DC, Maryland, West Virginia, Kentucky, Delaware, and Tennessee
>   4. Northeast: Pennsylvania, New Jersey, New York, Connecticut, Rhode Island, Massachusetts, Vermont, New Hampshire, and Maine.

• **tracts** Small, relatively permanent areas into which metropolitan and certain other areas are divided for the purpose of providing statistics for small areas. When census tracts are established, they are designed to be homogeneous with respect to population characteristics, economic status, and living conditions. Tracts generally have between 2,500 and 8,000 residents.

• **undercount** The percent of Americans who did not answer the decennial census.

centroid Geographic points marking the approximate centers of populations of the 260,000 block groups and enumeration districts in the U.S.

choropleth maps Computer-generated maps that represent values with shading.

cluster A category assigned to a neighborhood based on the assumption that the households share certain demographic, social, and economic characteristics.

cluster analysis The process of categorizing neighborhoods by lumping together such characteristics as income, age, housing types, education, and occupation. Cluster analysis assumes that averages describe the households in a neighborhood.

cohort A group of people who experience the same significant demographic event (birth, marriage) during a specific short time period, usually a year, and who can thus be identified as a group in subsequent analysis.

cohort measures Analysis of the activity of a cohort over an extended time period.

Consolidated Metropolitan Statistical Area (CMSA) A cluster of primary metropolitan statistical areas, such as Miami-Fort Lauderdale.

consumer expenditure What consumers spend on goods and services.

Consumer Price Index (CPI) The CPI compares the current cost of purchasing a fixed set of goods and services with the cost of the same set at a specific base year. The resulting measures can be compared over time.

concentric circle The shape of a geometric study area, sometimes referred to as a ring.

congressional districts The 435 congressional districts are defined by state legislatures for the purpose of electing persons to the U.S. House of Representatives.

Consumer Expenditure Survey (CEX) Data gathered in an ongoing survey by the Bureau of Labor Statistics on the expenditures of consumer units.

Consumer Information System Consumers generate four types of information of importance to businesses: demographics, lifestyles, media preferences, and purchasing behavior. By linking this information together, companies can build a complete picture of the consumer to analyze products, define markets, target advertising, and plan marketing strategies.

consumer unit All related members of a particular household; a person living alone or as a roomer, or sharing a household with others, who is financially independent; two or more persons living together who pool their incomes to make joint purchases, as defined by the Consumer Expenditure Survey.

Current Population Survey (CPS) The CPS is how the Census Bureau monitors changes between the decennial censuses. Each month, CPS interviewers ask people in about 60,000 households about their employment-related activities during the preceding week. The results provide marketers with up-to-date estimates of population size and characteristics.

D

Data User News A monthly newsletter issued by the U.S. Census Bureau which keeps data users informed about new products, census and survey plans, improvements in services from the bureau and State Data Centers and other program developments that may affect data users.

daytime population The population of an area during the daytime, which is usually far different from the residential population measured by the census. Businesses that are daytime-oriented—banks, auto repair shops, laundries, etc.—need to know where a given population is during the day in order to know where to locate or expand, and what products, services, and price levels to offer.

decennial census The census that is conducted by the U.S. Census Bureau every ten years in a year ending in a "0."

demography/demographics A social science concerned with the size, distribution, structure, and change of populations.

diary panel A survey in which the same respondents keep a diary of what they watch, listen to, or buy, etc., over a period of up to several weeks.

digitizing The process of assigning latitude and longitude coordinates for each twist and turn of a market area that is to be studied.

discretionary income See *income*.

disposable income See *income*.

DMA (Designated Marketing Area) A television market, as defined by NPD/ Nielsen, a firm which measures TV audiences. (See *television market*.)

E

emigration The process of leaving one country to live in another.

enumeration districts (EDs) Census enumeration areas, averaging around 500 inhabitants.

estimate An inference of the size of a population group or demographic characteristic based on a sample or another statistical method. Estimates are useful between the official counts produced by the decennial census.

family A group of two or more persons, one of them the householder, related by birth, marriage, or adoption and residing together.

fertility See *birth rate*.

focus group A qualitative market research method in which a topic is discussed by ten or fewer people led by a trained moderator.

forecast A projection which is believed likely to occur. *Forecasts* and *projections* are terms that are often used interchangeably, and many official agencies see little difference between the two.

G

geocoding (or geographic encoding) The process whereby addresses are segmented by county, MSA, postal route, etc., in order to compare them with information about the demographics and psychographics of those geographies. Geocoding is integral to demographically-enhanced mailing lists and cluster analysis.

geodemographic segmentation system See *cluster analysis*.

geography The geographic characteristics of a study area:
- **postal areas** Zip codes
- **political areas** States, counties, cities
- **census areas** Metropolitan Statistical Areas, census tracts, block groups, enumeration districts
- **telephone areas** Area codes and three-digit prefix calling areas
- **media marketing areas** ADIs and DMAs.

geometric study area A market site in the shape of a concentric circle or polygon that is to be analyzed. Private data companies use the data available for standard political and census geography to approximate the data for a geometric study area.

group quarters population Residents of military barracks, college dormitories, prisons, long-term-care hospitals, boarding houses, nursing homes, and the like.

H

household All the persons who occupy a housing unit.

householder In most cases, the person in whose name the home is owned or rented; formerly called head of household. In some cases, the individual who was surveyed or interviewed.

housing unit A house, apartment, group of rooms, or a single room occupied as separate living quarters.

I

immigration Movement into a country from another country.

income
- **gross** The total amount of money people have before taxes and necessities are paid for.
- **disposable** The income available to persons for spending or saving after taxes have been deducted.
- **discretionary** The amount of money people have for spending after taxes and necessities are paid for.
- **mean (or average)** This is derived by dividing the total income of a population by the population.
- **median** The amount of income which divides the distribution into two equal groups, one with an income above the median and the other with an income below the median.
- **money** Earnings, interest, dividends, royalties, net rental income, Social Security payments, and money from public assistance; i.e., all of the money people receive before they pay personal income taxes, Social Security taxes, and union dues.
- **per capita** The average amount of income per person in a population, regardless of age or labor force status. It is derived by dividing the total income by the total population.
- **personal** Money income plus certain noncash benefits.
- **types of** As defined by the Census Bureau: wage or salary income; nonfarm self-employment income; farm self-employment income; interest, dividend, or net rental income; Social Security income; public assistance income; all other income, which includes unemployment compensation, veterans' payment, pensions, alimony, etc.

inmigration Movement of people from one part of a country to another part of the same country.

L

labor force All civilians who are working or actively looking for work, plus members of the Armed Forced stationed in the U.S.

labor force participation rates The ratio of the population working or looking for work in an age-sex category to the total population in the category.

long census form The decennial census questionnaire that was answered by a sample of the population. Data from the long form are available only for large geographic areas because the Census Bureau has promised to protect the anonymity of all respondents.

longitudinal survey A long-term survey based on repeated analysis of either the same sample (called a panel study) or new samples chosen at regular intervals.

M

mapping The process by which a computer generates thematic maps that combine geography with demographic information and a company's sales data or other proprietary information.

Metropolitan Statistical Area (MSA) A free-standing metropolitan area surrounded by non-metropolitan counties and not closely associated with other metropolitan areas. Each MSA is grouped by population size: Those with a population of 1 million or more are in the "A" group; those with a population of 250,000 to 1 million are in the "B" group; those with a population of 100,000 to 250,000 are in "C" areas; and "D" areas are those with a population of less than 100,000.

microdata Census records of individual respondents stripped of their identifying information. Census microdata are available as public-use microdata samples (PUMS).

migration Movement of residence from one political area to another.

minor civil division A political and administrative subdivision of a county, generally a township.

mobility Geographic movement involving a change of residence.

modeling The formulation of mathematically-expressed variables to simulate a business decision environment. For example, a model could be formulated using demographics, local business conditions, the competition, and a company's financial data to select new markets that have the same winning combination of factors that are present in currently successful markets.

mortality Deaths.

N

nonfamily household A household comprised of a person living alone or with nonrelatives, as defined by the Census Bureau.

O

outmigration Movement from a given area into another part of the same country.

P

panel survey A survey in which the same respondents are interviewed several times over an extended period; also called longitudinal analysis.

polygon The shape of a geometric study area.

population The number of people who are in a certain area on a certain date.
 • **density** A measure that is computed by dividing the total population of a geographic unit by its land area measured in square miles or square kilometers.
 • **estimate** A calculation of the current population between decennial censuses, arrived at by a variety of methods.
 • **growth rate** The total increase or decrease in a population during a given period divided by the average population in that period.

population pyramid The graphic representation of a population's age-sex composition. It is a bar graph with the population divided into ages or age groups, represented from the youngest at the bottom to the oldest at the top, with males on the left and females on the right.

postal carrier routes/postal code Zip codes.

poverty The income cutoffs used by the Census Bureau to determine the poverty status of families and unrelated individuals, based on family size. The poverty thresholds are revised annually to allow for changes in the cost of living as reflected in the Consumer Price Index.

Primary Metropolitan Statistical Area (PMSA) A metropolitan area that is adjacent to another.

projection An estimate, based on assumptions about future trends in births, deaths, and migration, of a demographic characteristic such as population or number of households.

psychographics Lifestyle research.

Q

qualitative research Research characterized by the absence of empirical measurements and an interest in subjective evaluations; e.g., focus groups.

quantitative research Research conducted for the purpose of obtaining empirical evaluations of attitudes, behavior, or performance. Most quantitative research is based on information supplied by a relatively small group that is representative of a larger population.

R

random sampling A sample in which each unit has an equal and independent chance of selection.

rate The number of occurrences of an event, such as death, divided by the population at risk of dying.

ratio A measure that expresses the relative size of two numbers.

regional marketing Marketing aimed at local rather than national markets.

rural population As defined by the 1980 census, those areas not classified as urban. (See *urban population*.)

rustbelt States in the Great Lakes region whose economies suffered during the late 1970s, causing many of their residents to move to other states.

S

sampling The method of selecting a specified portion, called a sample, from a population, from which information concerning the whole can be inferred.

sampling error The estimated inaccuracy of the results of a study when a population sample is used to explain behavior of the total population.

separate living quarters Those in which the occupants live and eat separately from other persons in the building and have direct access from the outside of the building or through a common hall.

sex ratio The number of males per 100 females in a population.

short census form The decennial census questionnaire that all Americans answered, or were supposed to answer.

site evaluation Determining, through an analysis of a given area's demographic and economic characteristics, whether it offers a good market for a product or service.

snowbirds People who are temporary residents of an area; e.g., retirees who spend the winter in Florida.

social indicator A numerical measure of the quality of life.

state data center An organization within a state, generally a planning agency, university, or library, to which the Census Bureau furnishes products, training in data access and use, technical assistance, and consultation. The data center in turn disseminates the products to the public and provides assistance with their use in the state.

Summary Tape Files (STFs) These 1980 computer tapes, organized according to subject and geography, contain a broad range of population and housing data from the short and long decennial census forms.

sunbelt As defined by the Census Bureau, it is the Census Regions South and West. According to American Demographics magazine and many marketers, it is the 13 states that are entirely below the 37th parallel, plus one county in Nevada and nine counties in California that are also below the belt, and, of course, Hawaii.

T

telephone sample A group of randomly- or otherwise-selected people who are surveyed by telephone.

television market This term is best defined by an example: Pike County, Pennsylvania, is located 100 miles from Philadelphia and 100 miles from New York City. Pike County falls into the New York television market because the largest share of viewing in Pike County is tuned to New York stations. The two firms which measure TV audiences, Arbitron and NPD/Nielsen, have slightly different definitions of television markets, based on sampling, etc. Arbitron's TV markets are called Areas of Dominant Influence (ADIs), while Nielsen's are Designated Market Areas, or DMAs.

temporary population Tourists, commuters, "snowbirds," and other temporary residents of an area.

thematic maps Computer-generated maps that combine geography with demographic data and company information on sales, etc.

time use survey A survey of how people use their time, taken by asking people to record what they do and how they do it in a diary over several days or weeks.

trade area The geographical area from which the customers of a business are drawn; it can be as small as a section of a city or as large as the entire country.

U

urban population As defined by the 1980 census, all persons living in urbanized areas and in places of 2,500 or more inhabitants outside urbanized areas.

urbanized areas A central city or cities and the surrounding closely settled territory or "urban fringe."

V

variance The statistical measure of how similar a population is in a characteristic being studied.

Z

zip code demographics The demographic characteristics of a population living in a particular zip code.

INDEX

B

C

I

M

P

Y

Z